The Neuroscience *of* Reading Music

*Optimal Brain Development in Children
Using Standard Music Notation*

Barbara A. Moir, M. Ed.

THE NEUROSCIENCE OF READING MUSIC: OPTIMAL BRAIN DEVELOPMENT IN CHILDREN USING STANDARD MUSIC NOTATION

Copyright © 2025 Barbara A. Moir, M. Ed.

1210 SW 23rd PL • Ocala, FL 34471 • Phone 352-622-1825
Website: www.atlantic-pub.com • Email: sales@atlantic-pub.com
SAN Number: 268-1250

No part of this publication may be reproduced, stored in a retrieval system, or transmitted in any form or by any means, electronic, mechanical, photocopying, recording, scanning, or otherwise, except as permitted under Section 107 or 108 of the 1976 United States Copyright Act, without the prior written permission of the Publisher. Requests to the Publisher for permission should be sent to Atlantic Publishing Group, Inc., 1210 SW 23rd PL, Ocala, Florida 34471.

Library of Congress Control Number: 2025901520

LIMIT OF LIABILITY/DISCLAIMER OF WARRANTY: The publisher and the author make no representations or warranties with respect to the accuracy or completeness of the contents of this work and specifically disclaim all warranties, including without limitation warranties of fitness for a particular purpose. No warranty may be created or extended by sales or promotional materials. The advice and strategies contained herein may not be suitable for every situation. This work is sold with the understanding that the publisher is not engaged in rendering legal, accounting, or other professional services. If professional assistance is required, the services of a competent professional should be sought. Neither the publisher nor the author shall be liable for damages arising herefrom. The fact that an organization or website is referred to in this work as a citation and/or a potential source of further information does not mean that the author or the publisher endorses the information the organization or website may provide or recommendations it may make. Further, readers should be aware that Internet websites listed in this work may have changed or disappeared between when this work was written and when it is read.

TRADEMARK DISCLAIMER: All trademarks, trade names, or logos mentioned or used are the property of their respective owners and are used only to directly describe the products being provided. Every effort has been made to properly capitalize, punctuate, identify, and attribute trademarks and trade names to their respective owners, including the use of ® and ™ wherever possible and practical. Atlantic Publishing Group, Inc. is not a partner, affiliate, or licensee with the holders of said trademarks.

Printed in the United States

PROJECT MANAGER: Crystal Edwards
INTERIOR LAYOUT AND JACKET DESIGN: Nicole Sturk

*Dedicated to
young children
everywhere
who read music notation
and the instructors
who guide them.*

Table of Contents

Introduction 1

Chapter 1: Exploring the Landscape of Music Cognition 3

Diversity Within the Music Model 3

How Gardner Viewed Music Diversity 5

Seeking Gardner's "Plurality of Mechanisms" 5

Chapter 2: Natural Abilities Versus Trained Abilities 9

Musical Abilities of Infants and Toddlers 9

Components of Spatial Intelligence 11

Spatial Recognition 11

Spatial Recognition in the General Classroom 12

Spatial Transformation 14

Spatial Transformation on the Game Board 14

Spatial Transformation in Reading Music 15

Spatial Transformation in Reading Words 16

Defining Music Cognition 16

Is Something Still Missing? 17

Chapter 3: Closing the Gaps 19
How the Third Mode Works 20
Examples from the Classroom 21
Defining All Three Modes 23
Linking Mode and Professional Instrumentalists 23

Chapter 4: Steady Beat 25
Three Types of Steady Beat Abilities in Each Mode 25
How the Musician Experiences Steady Beat 26
Professional Standards for Steady Beat 28
Steady Beat for School Children 29
Research in Steady Beat Abilities 30
The Criteria for Whole Body Coordination 31
How the Brain Regulates Steady Beat 31
Other Uses For Steady Beat 33
Connecting Steady Beat to Cognitive Development 33
Methods that Develop Large Motor Responses to Music .. 35
Steady Beat and the Three Modes 36

Chapter 5: Tenets of Aural Mode 37
Brief Outline of Aural Mode 37
Intelligences Needed for Aural Mode 39
Requirements for Conformity in Aural Mode 40
Singing "On-pitch?" 40
More About Formal Pitch Training 42

Table of Contents

Chapter 6: Tenets of Notational Mode **45**

    Brief Outline of Notational Mode 46

    Research of Spatial and Kinesthetic Neurons 50

    Spatial Skills begin in PreK 51

    Comprehensive Note Reading in Early Grades 52

    Major Considerations in Notational Mode 53

    How Does the Teacher Learn the Order of Skills? 53

Chapter 7: Hierarchy in Notational Mode **57**

    Operational Hierarchy in Standard Notation 58

    The Hierarchy of Rhythm in Instrumental Music 59

    Two Types of Hierarchy in Level 1 Rhythms 59

    Reinforcing the Student's Perception of Hierarchy 60

    Operational Hierarchy in Structured Music 60

    Boosting Students' Ability to Count While Playing 62

    A Trick to Build a Student's Counting Ability 63

    A Spatial Intelligence Method for Reading Rhythm 64

    The Loop Counting System 67

    Hierarchy in Pitch Knowledge 68

    Hierarchy in Review 69

Chapter 8: Abstraction and Symbolism **71**

    Piano Lessons for PreK Students 71

    What's the Hurry? 72

    New Solutions Overcoming Abstractions 73

    The Companion Words Method 74

    Three Components of a Musical Symbol 75

    Abstract Concepts through Companion Words 78

    The 2015 Amherst Study for Hierarchy 79

    Implications for Early Childhood Education 80

    Teaching Abstractions in Early Childhood 81

    Teaching Music Symbols in Early Childhood 82

    The Companion Words Script 82

    Time Requirements for Companion Words 83

Chapter 9: The Importance of Process 85

    Kinesthetic Training that Precedes the All-At-Once Method 86

    Why Piano Students Begin Differently 87

    Processing Notation for the First Time 87

    Remediating Deficiencies in Reading Music 90

    Understanding Order in the Reading Process 92

    Local Skills at the Staff Level 93

    Local Skills at the Instrument Level 94

    Remedies for Weak Spatial Skills on the Instrument 95

    Other Technical Issues that Require Drill 97

    Spatial Transformation from Staff to Instrument 97

        Four Different Types of Transformations 98

    The "Backwards" Method for Teaching the Staff 100

    Final Thoughts About Processes in Reading Music 100

Chapter 10: Training the Eyes 103

    Eye Motion Levels in Reading Music 103

    Improving Eye Motion Abilities 104

    An Exercise for Better Eye Motion 107

    Reading Groups of Tones 108

    Fostering Better Reading Methods 110

Chapter 11: Alphabetic Logic 111

    What is Fixed Order? 112

    The Origins of Fixed Alphabetic Order 113

    Our Innate Abilities for Alphabetic Logic 114

    The Role of Alphabetic Logic in Reading Music 115

    Alternating between Shapes and Letter Names 118

    Introducing Alphabetic Scanning Skills 119

        Four Alphabetic Scanning Skills 120

    Adjacency of Letters Within the Fixed Order 120

    How Alphabetic Adjacency Affects Scanning Skills 121

        Stepwise Movement (or Basic Adjacency) 121

        Clustered (Adjacent) Letters 121

        Skipping (An Advanced Form of Adjacency) 122

        Neighboring Tones (Adjacency in Both Directions) 123

    Other Teaching Tips for Alphabetic Skills 123

    Final Thoughts on Alphabetic Logic 124

Chapter 12: Tenets of Linking Mode 125

Technical Accuracy and Musical Expression 125

The Order of Tasks in Linking Mode 128

Interpretive Practices in Classrooms 129

My Personal Quest for the Secrets of Musical Expression 130

Applications of Linking Mode 131

Examples of Interpretive Learning *132*

Final Thoughts on Linking Mode 136

Chapter 13: Chronic Mistakes Syndrome 139

Battling The Elusive Demon 139

Why Is It Called A Syndrome? 140

The Cause Of This Syndrome 141

What is *The Scatter Technique*? 142

How to Use *The Scatter Technique* 143

Variations of *The Scatter Technique* 144

Long Term Effects of Chronic Mistakes Syndrome 145

How Well Does *The Scatter Technique* Work? 146

Chapter 14: Language, Literacy, And Reading Music 147

Reading Words 148

Abstractions in Reading *148*

Eye Techniques in Reading *149*

Giving Children Time to Grow *151*

Omitting Spatial Intelligence Training *151*

Other Language Arts *151*

Math And Spatial Intelligence 153
    Math Calculations and Music... 153
    Math Word Problems and Music 154
How Reading Affects the Broader Curriculum 155
A Personal Story About Spatial Training 155
New Aural Trends About to Impact Secondary Ensembles 157

Chapter 15: Effective Notational Reading Programs 159

Practical Considerations for Establishing a Notational
Music Program 160
The Importance of Review During Each Year 163
Sight Reading in Early Grades.. 163
Music Dictation is Useful at Any Level 164
Lesson Ideas for The Three-Five Pitch Plan 165
    Notational Strategies for PreK.. 165
    Notational Strategies for Kindergarten 166
    Notational Strategies for First and Second Grades 167
    Notational Strategies for Third Grade 169
Nothing Happens Without Steady Beat... 171

Chapter 16: Notational Reading Goals for Music Literacy 173

Foundational Skills for Music Literacy.. 173

Chapter 17: Future Research In Music 177

Ten Topics for Study 177

Chapter 18: The Promise of Tomorrow 181

ADDENDUMS

Addendum 1: Guide to Understanding the 2015 Amherst Study 185

Addendum 2: National Music Goals in Relation to Reading Music 187

Addendum 3: Aural Myths in General Music 191

Addendum 4: The Loop System of Counting 195

    Clapping the Loops 197

    Drawing the Loops 199

    Advantages of Loops 199

Addendum 5: Classroom Management for Student Xylophone Lessons 201

Addendum 6: Introducing Companion Words in Early Childhood 205

    Poster-by-Poster Script for Introducing Companion Words 206

    Small Nuances that Improve Companion Words 217

    The Concept of "Location" in Early Lessons 219

Addendum 7: Classroom Example of Lap-to-Instrument Technique 221

Addendum 8: The Backwards Method 223

Addendum 9: Keeping the "Fun" in Learning Alphabetic Adjacency 227

Select Bibliography 229

    Books 229

    Articles 230

    Websites for National Standards in Education 232

Acknowledgments 233

About the Author 235

Introduction

It is my core belief that every young child deserves the chance to read music—not simply for the purpose of entertainment or cultural enrichment (although both of those goals are highly commendable), but to develop their brains to their full capacity early on when it matters most—while the brain is still growing.

Lately, when I read the results of national testing surveys and learn that almost half of eighth graders in inner city schools are reading below grade level, I have to wonder whether a keyboard class for reading music taken once a day throughout their high school freshman year wouldn't correct many of their learning problems. The ability to recognize shapes, distance, and direction of written objects such as notation on the music staff assists the student in using necessary skills for recognizing alphabet letters, word shapes, placement of numbers in long division or multiplication, and so much more. From my experience in both the music and academic classroom, the most prolific way to train the eyes and brain is through reading music notation—as demonstrated in this book.

Up until now, we may have believed that children under the age of seven were not good candidates for reading music as their brains were not mature in the area of processing abstract information. In this book, I aim to show that the only abstract part of music notation is the adult names we have assigned to the music symbols. By using a new system for introducing notation called *Companion Words*, children can quickly learn to use notation through age-appropriate terminology. This method has been classroom-tested and is backed by neural science. A complete script for this method is included in this book to help teachers instruct notation to students as young as four and five years old.

This book supports music literacy in our schools—with practical solutions.

Imagine our schools in the future if children had adequate working knowledge of the music staff by the end of the 3rd grade. Imagine the singing programs that could be developed for children who could read notation. Imagine the compositions children could write. Imagine 4th or 5th grade general music students performing their own written scores on stage.

In this ideal scenario, children who already possessed note-reading skills could make an informed decision as to whether or not they would like to join a band, orchestra, or chorus program. Some children from disadvantaged situations, where higher education might ordinarily have been deemed improbable, might break through their own economic barriers and become a teacher, simply through the opportunity at school to excel at reading music. I am one such example. My parents weren't planning to send me to college until my music teacher convinced them I had shown great aptitude for music. I was the first in my family to attend college—a privilege that has since been passed on to my children and grandchildren.

Additionally, a notational reading program would positively empower students in the academic classroom during a time when technology and AI are replacing and diminishing cognitive abilities. We would have fewer at-risk students because reading standard music notation would equip every student with highly developed visual skills and spatial intelligence abilities.

Cognitive abilities through music is an area of education that I have been interested in all my life. It is with deep satisfaction that I now present this book to you as a formal record of the amazing tasks our brains can complete if we understand and implement the necessary training.

Chapter 1

Exploring the Landscape of Music Cognition

There are many differing opinions and unanswered questions about the value of reading music and its place in the school curriculum today. While we universally seem familiar with the role of music intelligence associated with natural abilities such as singing, pitch recognition, imitating, improvising, and listening to music and evaluating it—we know less about which intelligence has the greatest influence on formal skills for reading music.

The purpose of this book is to present a complete model for music and the brain that includes every type of music activity. I'll show you educational and scientific research studies, and I'll share my experiences in the classroom to illustrate true practical application.

Diversity Within the Music Model

A primary concept in my complete model of music cognition is that *aural abilities and formal notational abilities are processed in separate and very different parts of the brain.*

This can now be verified by the 2015 neurological study from the University of Massachusetts, Amherst by P. Taylor; J.N. Hobbs; J. Burroni; and H.T. Siegelmann entitled "The Global Landscape of Cognition: Hierarchical aggregation as an organizational principle of human cortical networks and functions." (*Scientific Reports*, December 2015). [Hereafter referred to as the 2015 Amherst Study.]

This groundbreaking study was never intended to be a music study, per se. These scientists merely set out to prove or disprove whether a hierarchy exists in the brain for processing various everyday skills. They measured how far information consistently traveled into the brain from cortical sensory inputs such as the ears or eyes. They also measured the length of the neural pathways that carried information.

Among their many findings, researchers reported that natural abilities in music such as *musical cognition, auditory discrimination, music comprehension/production, pitch, prosody, musical tones, and auditory perception* (the primary focus of elementary general music programs) use the *shortest neural pathways* on the first tier of the brain's hierarchy. Conversely, skills such as *symbolism, abstractions, and naming* (all of which are essential for reading music as well as English literacy and math) use the *longest neural pathways*, at the fifth and highest level of cognition.

In other words, conductors who read musical scores, professional instrumentalists who sight read, and students who read music in ensembles and private lessons are all developing the long neural pathways for abstractions, symbolism, and naming. Conversely, musicians who engage in music without reading notation (those who play by ear, imitate, or listen to music) are developing the shortest neurological pathways, according to the 2015 Amherst Study.

This is relatively new information that schools have not yet taken advantage of when it comes to helping children develop more complex forms of cognition.

We'll return to the 2015 Amherst Study again later in **Chapter 8:** *Abstraction and Symbolism*. But if you'd like to examine the study for yourself, see **Addendum 1:** *Guide to Understanding the 2015 Amherst Study* for information that will help you find the study online and direct you to the music information within the study.

How Gardner Viewed Music Diversity

Longer and shorter neural pathways are only one of the ways aural and notational abilities differ. To find other differences, we need to return to a book published back in 1983—the book that first gave us all the information about music intelligence and spurred our interest in music and the brain. I'm referring, of course, to Harvard Professor Howard Gardner's *Frames of Mind, the Theory of Multiple Intelligences*.

Over many decades, Gardner's book became a standard reference in education. And, surprisingly, I've found it holds even more answers today for music than we originally thought possible. Most of us who read *Frames of Mind* came away with a good understanding of aural skills and music intelligence, but when it came to music skills such as reading notation, Gardner did not commit to any direct link between formal notational abilities and specific areas of the brain. We were left—more or less—to guess if notational skills were also part of music intelligence. I think many educators assumed they were.

Ultimately, Gardner did provide the information we need about formal abilities—you just have to know where to find it.

Seeking Gardner's "Plurality of Mechanisms"

When Gardner coined the term *music intelligence* in the 1980s with his book *Frames of Mind*, it had a huge impact on music education. For the first time, we learned that a specific physical part of the brain was dedicated to music abilities. Gardner's new term provided teachers with the impetus to approach their administrators and school boards and say, "See, this is why we have to teach music in our schools. Music ability requires using a portion of the brain that can't be trained through other disciplines. It requires specialized training and specialized instructors. Otherwise, the music section of a child's brain will remain undeveloped."

Educators still reference *Frames of Mind* today for designing many types of curricula to stimulate and develop all parts of the brain. Current neurological studies also refer to Gardner's intelligences in their published reports.

In the beginning of *Frames of Mind*, Gardner reviews older theories of multiple intelligences before presenting his own model, which he based on medical reports and studies on brain injuries that link distinct behaviors to specific physical regions of the brain. Gardner's *Frames of Mind* originally identified seven different intelligences in the human brain: **linguistic, musical, logical-mathematical, spatial, bodily-kinesthetic, and two personal intelligences.**

Even though I greatly appreciated Gardner's theories, I always thought there was one drawback to his chapter on music intelligence. While it offered a great deal of information about singing, birdsong, and aural aspects of music, it said less about visual music skills such as reading music performed on a musical instrument—skills he referred to as *formal training*. By the end of his chapter on music intelligence, he leaves us to assume that all music skills (aural and visual) belong in the same category of music intelligence because he provides no information to the contrary.

To be fair, I don't blame Gardner for being vague about the origins of formal music skills because he was not a professional music educator. Reading notation is so highly technical that understanding it requires personal knowledge and experience that, in my opinion, few researchers possess.

However, to his credit, Gardner freely admitted his discoveries were only tapping the surface of our musical abilities. Notice, too, what he said in *Frames of Mind*:

> "... [there is a] tremendous range of types and degrees of musical skill found in the human population; since individuals differ so much in what they can do, it is conceivable that the nervous

system can offer a plurality of mechanisms for carrying out these performances."

It is precisely these "plurality of mechanisms" that we have not yet defined or explored in music. For instance, how many mechanisms are there? What titles or names would we assign to them? How do they each work?

Without proper labels, scientists are unable to articulate which mechanism is being researched. Teachers can't reference these mechanisms when writing curriculum for the music classroom or speak to their students about which mechanism they are developing. Parents can't request that schools teach all the mechanisms in music because, other than music intelligence (up until the publication of this book), these mechanisms have remained unknown.

That's why we have to go back to Gardner's chapter on music intelligence to find the clues. But this time, instead of blindly accepting his conclusions, we need to weigh them against all we know about early childhood development. In doing so, we'll find a new path for music that leads away from music intelligence to other important parts of the brain.

Chapter 2

Natural Abilities Versus Trained Abilities

The first statement in Gardner's chapter on music intelligence is a perfect example of incorrectly lumping all music activities and behaviors into one music category, without regard to the diverse processes involved.

Gardner states, "Of all the gifts with which individuals may be endowed, none emerges earlier than musical talent."

On its face, this statement is partly true. While Gardner is correct that *aural musical talent* emerges early, *other musical talents do not*. In fact, they don't "emerge" at all—they must be specifically trained.

Musical Abilities of Infants and Toddlers

To identify which music abilities emerge early (and which do not), we can simply look at the behaviors of babies and toddlers.

For instance, we know that babies vocalize and imitate sounds as a means of communication, almost from birth. At eighteen months to two years old, some toddlers can sing simple nursery songs. By the time my daughter was two years old, I had compiled a list of more than thirty titles of short songs she could sing. So, the ability of some babies and toddlers to vocalize and express meaning through music agrees with Gardner's opening statement about musical talent emerging early.

On the other hand, babies and toddlers are not born with the ability to read quarter notes or use alphabet letters on the music staff; nor are they capable of arranging their fingers on finger holes of an instrument. The music staff and the musical instrument are vehicles for performing music from the printed page. The abilities to use these vehicles do not emerge on their own.

This is quite evident when we observe young children trying to place their fingers on the holes of soprano recorders or toy flutes for the first time. Even when we show children exactly how to hold the instrument and where to place their fingers, they lack the fine motor coordination to keep their fingers in place or lift individual fingers. They are also unable to *understand* or *remember* finger patterns for covering certain holes.

Furthermore, even when babies and toddlers can demonstrate their natural music ability to vocalize high or low pitches, they lack the ability to recognize or remember which direction on the instrument will produce sounds that go higher or lower.

They also lack the ability to visually recognize shapes, distance, and direction on the music staff. They haven't learned to recognize geometric shapes. They lack the ability to count lines or identify them as "line one" or "the second line." And the notion that the space between lines is real and usable is far too abstract for the infant/toddler mind.

Because these skills do not "emerge" on their own but rather must be trained, we can safely assume the neural pathways for *trained* music abilities are *undeveloped* at birth. In order to master these technical skills, the neural pathways must be introduced and strengthened through guidance and repetition.

Gardner was not able to conclusively explain the origins of these formal music abilities in his chapter on music intelligence. However, two chapters later, he unknowingly did exactly that through a math-related topic that aligns perfectly with almost every aspect of trained formal music abilities—*spatial intelligence*. And, as you will see later, the use of spatial intelligence in music opens the door to unmistakable similarities between the skills used for reading music and those required for academic subjects.

Components of Spatial Intelligence

In his book, Gardner discusses many aspects of spatial intelligence, but curiously never summarizes or groups these abilities. So, when I went back to look for information related to music, the first thing I did was to condense his view of spatial intelligence into four easily referenced components. I call them the Four Principles of Spatial Intelligence that directly apply to learning in school:

> **Spatial Intelligence Principle #1**: The *recognition* of objects in space according to shape, distance, and direction
>
> **Spatial Intelligence Principle #2**: The *transformation* of one element into another
>
> **Spatial Intelligence Principle #3**: The *ability to conjure* up and transform mental imagery
>
> **Spatial Intelligence Principle #4**: The ability to produce a *"graphic likeness of spatial information."*

It's evident how Principles 3 and 4, *mental imagery* and *graphic likeness*, would relate to drawing and painting—even to writing music notation. But Principles 1 and 2, *recognition* and *transformation*, are vital to all aspects of reading from the music staff and transferring that information to an instrument.

Spatial Recognition

A perfect illustration of our ability to recognize objects in space by their **shape, distance,** or **direction** was provided by Gardner in his example of map reading.

We *recognize* objects (cities, rivers) by their *shape* on the map, by *distances* from surrounding objects, and by their *direction* (north or south) compared to other objects.

Similarly, I've discovered that, in reading music, we use the first principle of spatial intelligence to recognize information about notes on the music staff by their *shape* (whether they are white or shaded in; whether they have stems, beams, or flags), by their *distances* (intervals) from other notes written before or after; and by their *direction* on the music staff (ascending or descending).

Spatial Recognition in the General Classroom

There are many similar examples of spatial recognition (by shape, distance, and direction) in the reading of words.

In learning alphabet letters, spatial recognition helps the student identify each letter's shape as a combination of straight lines or curved lines. The letter O is all curved. The capital A and capital E are made up of all straight lines. The letters B or D use straight and curved lines.

Alphabet letters are also defined by *distance* factors. The lines on an upper case K are drawn a farther distance with a pencil than for the lower case k. The same is true for upper and lower case w's, x's, y's, and z's.

Spatial recognition of *direction* is also important in the identification of the lower case b and d. Are the curved portions located on the right or the left of the letter?

But this is only the beginning. Spatial recognition takes on an even greater role when alphabet shapes are combined to form words and sentences.

First, young readers must first develop the spatial intelligence knowledge that helps them distinguish which direction to send their eyes. They must learn to read from left to right on the page, from the top of the page to the bottom, and from pages on the left to pages on the right.

Students also use spatial intelligence knowledge as they begin to form words and sentences. For example, they may review their writing assignments by making sure they have used capital letters at the beginning of every sentence (tall letters recognized by shape and distance). They may look for periods or question marks at the end of each sentence (more shape recognition). If they are studying how to write indented paragraphs, they will use spatial intelligence to determine how far to indent the first line. And of course, they use spatial intelligence when they print letters and words with their pencil. But even those who use a keyboard must recognize the letters by their shape, distance, and direction. For that matter, the ability to find the location of each alphabetic key on the keyboard also depends on an awareness of how the keys are positioned in relation to each other—a clear use of spatial intelligence.

Later in the book, I will show you the many ways these same types of spatial *recognition*, as well as *transformation* abilities, are essential for understanding math word problems and writing math calculations. Since reading and math are required for the social and biological sciences, we can safely assume that spatial intelligence plays a major role in mastering those subjects as well.

The first principle of spatial intelligence is required for art class, in which students use shape, distance, and direction to express ideas through original artwork.

Spatial intelligence is also required in physical education where the ability to judge distance and direction is paramount in all sports activities.

In summary, it would be difficult to find any subject in school that is not dependent on spatial recognition skills. Why not, then, boost children's spatial intelligence awareness right away the first year of school by introducing age-appropriate tasks in one of the most prolific subjects for developing spatial intelligence—the reading and writing of standard music notation?

Spatial Transformation

Gardner described *spatial transformation* as our ability to transform one element into another element. However, I don't think the word 'element' fully conveys what Gardner really meant. Most of us think of an element as something with physical properties, such as elements on the Periodic Table (like hydrogen or oxygen). For purposes of clarity in our discussion of music, I am going to replace his word 'element' with the words "*system of thought.*" Here in this book, we will talk about the ability to transform one *system of thought* to another *system of thought*, without losing the value or meaning during the transformation. In doing so, I believe we will remain true to Gardner's intended definition of transformative abilities in spatial intelligence.

Spatial Transformation on the Game Board

It's easy to visualize spatial transformation if you examine the steps for each player's turn on a board game. First, the player rolls the dice. The player uses spatial *recognition* to identify the dots as circle *shapes* on the top of the two cubes.

Next, the player switches to the second type of spatial intelligence—*transformation*—to spatially *transform* geometric shape information (dot-dot-dot-dot) to logical-math information (the number "four").

Then the player uses spatial *transformation* again to spatially *transform* "four" to a visual two-dimensional pattern—four squares on the game board.

The player finishes the process by switching back to spatial *recognition* to decide the *direction* to move the game piece.

During this board game, did the value of the information remain constant? Yes. The player started with four dots and ended up with four squares on the board. Spatial transformation is exact and absolute. The system and its appearance may change, but the value remains intact.

Spatial Transformation in Reading Music

By understanding how we use spatial intelligence to play a board game, we can easily visualize a similar use of spatial intelligence during the note reading process.

Let's examine an example wherein a reader spatially *recognizes* that two black notes (circle shapes known as note heads) on the music staff proceed upward from a line to the next space. The reader spatially *transforms* this visual image into two different types of spatial knowledge. One is *direction* (upward movement), and the other is *distance* (the idea of close proximity between the line and space, with no room in between).

Shape, distance, and *direction* must then be spatially *transformed* to the mechanical system of the instrument, be it piano keys, guitar frets, finger holes, valves, or slide system. The reader uses the idea of direction to make sure the two tones move upward. And uses the idea of distance (proximity) to make sure the tones are next to each other on the instrument. The shape of the notes on the staff also shows the reader how long the sounds should be played (duration).

So, the performer recognizes and transforms information about shape (duration), direction, and distance on the music staff to mechanical knowledge on the instrument, all at once, for every note in a piece of music.

Is spatial transformation exact and absolute in notational reading? Yes. A single and specific location on the lines and spaces refers to one—and only one—place on the instrument (or one place on an individual string of a string instrument). Going upward on the staff means moving upward in pitch on the instrument. Four tones in succession on the staff will result in four tones in succession on the instrument. A music symbol that represents four beats on the staff will mean four beats of sound on the instrument. And so forth.

Spatial Transformation in Reading Words

How does spatial transformation look when the information is in printed words instead of written on the music staff?

Transformation in reading occurs as the written letters of the word are associated with and transformed into a corresponding remembered *image*, silent *meaning*, or *vocal pronunciation* already stored in the reader's mind.

Defining Music Cognition

We've just considered the role of spatial intelligence on a game board, in reading music, and in the general school curriculum. Now let's see how these spatial abilities compare to music intelligence abilities found in music activities.

Gardner specifically defined *music intelligence* as "the ability of individuals to discern *meaning* and *importance* in sets of pitches rhythmically arranged and also to produce such metrically arranged pitch sequences as a means of communicating with other individuals."

In other words, *music intelligence*:

- uses *aural* skills to recognize and arrange pitches;
- assigns meaning to arranged sets of pitches;
- communicates personal and cultural meaning (joy, sadness, ceremony, storytelling, etc.) to others through metrically arranged pitch sequences.

Whereas *spatial intelligence*:

- uses *visual* recognition of shapes, distances and direction;
- transforms technical visual information from the printed page to a mechanical musical instrument.

Natural Abilities Versus Trained Abilities

Admittedly, the Amherst study that measured the short and long neurons does not specifically use the term "spatial intelligence" anywhere in the study; however, I believe we must take a step forward here and conclude that spatial intelligence is the accurate term to describe the information that travels on the long neurons. Remember that spatial intelligence is defined as the ability to *recognize* the shapes, distance, and direction of symbols and to *translate* that information to the instrument—the exact skills needed to access the symbolism, naming, and abstractions of the long neurons listed in the Amherst study. (Obviously, there are other intelligences also involved in reading music, such as kinesthetic, mathematical, personal, and language intelligence. However, spatial intelligence is the primary force in reading music. So, for the sake of simplicity and clarity, I am presenting the most important details rather than all possible details.)

Then by referencing the Amherst study, we can divide music cognition into two modes of cognition—an aural system with music intelligence on the short neurons, and a visual system with spatial intelligence on the long neurons—Aural mode and Notational Mode.

Is Something Still Missing?

There is a musical ability that has never been well defined or understood in music education and that is the ability to go beyond mere decoding of notation to the skill of decoding in a meaningful and holistic manner. Would we assume that the long neurons for decoding also carry information for musical expression? So far, science has not supported that idea. The Amherst study showed that the long neurons only account for symbolism, naming, and abstractions, and other skills such as humor and imagination, while meaning through music is processed on the short neural pathways near the ears. It would appear then that reading music with expression requires some other type of processing in the brain that goes beyond simply using the long neurons for decoding.

Perhaps music research in the future will provide the answers we need. If electronic imaging were to measure the behavior of neural pathways at the moment a person is just decoding and then separately measure the neural pathways while a person is decoding and also processing musical expression, we would have a better understanding of the complex neural activity involved in musical expression.

Another good study would be to measure the brain activity of performers as they learn technique first, then add musical expression compared to learning methods that involve musical expression as soon as the note-reading process begins. Which method would result in strong, stable long neurons for note reading *and* the ability to add musical expression?

In our search for this special type of cognition that brings musical expression into the decoding process, we need to take into account that using musical expression is not an automatic result of learning to decode. I know from years of teaching music that some people never acquire the ability to incorporate elements of musical expression as they perform from printed music, instead only processing spatial intelligence on the long neurons and never connecting with music intelligence at all. Other people learn over time to add elements of musical expression once they can decode the notation and comfortably handle their musical instrument. The fact that decoding ability can be present with or without musical expression suggests that the brain has one process for decoding alone and a different process for decoding that incorporates music intelligence.

How does the brain connect music intelligence abilities with decoding of notation? This mystery qualifies as one of those unexplained "mechanisms" Gardner was referring to when defining music cognition.

Gardner also said that any *unexplained ability* in an educational or scientific theory is called a *gap*.

We have just found one.

Chapter 3

Closing the Gaps

Howard Gardner warns us to guard against theories that have gaps or areas that do not remain true to the model:

> ". . . there is something awry about a list that leaves glaring and obvious gaps, or one that fails to generate the vast majority of roles and skills valued by human cultures."

He is absolutely correct. When there is a gap in the way we view something, some elements do not make sense or cannot be explained. When music is defined only as singing, creating, listening, and evaluating music, we have left out those who create music by reading and writing music symbols. Similarly, when we say that reading music is only spatial intelligence or only processed on long neurons, we haven't explained how some read music in a musically expressive manner (which can't be explained through spatial abilities).

This leads me to believe the musician who produces holistic, meaningful sounds from printed music is using a third type of music cognition. This third and different mode allows the reader to tap into music intelligence while simultaneously using spatial intelligence to process music notation.

Thus, music cognition is not two different processes—but three. I call them *Aural,* *Notational,* and *Linking* modes.

How the Third Mode Works

The third mode of music cognition, *Linking Mode* (short for Aural-Notational Linking Mode), acts as a facilitator, bringing together spatial reading skills and aural memory. It's a sophisticated procedure that requires a number of *instantaneous* steps:

1. The brain recognizes the type or style of music being played at the moment, in real time (i.e. classical, jazz, pop, etc.);

2. The brain searches samples of music stored in music memory to find similar examples of the music being performed;

3. The brain brings the "found" music information into the reader's consciousness, allowing the reader to compare, change, and shape the sound to match the information retrieved from music intelligence.

For example, imagine a student is reading the music notation for a waltz, but the notes produced on the instrument sound choppy and awkward. The instructor reminds the student to remember how a waltz really sounds on the dance floor. After a moment of thought, the student begins again, this time playing smoothly with proper emphasis on first beats in measures, adding the flow and grace expected in a waltz. What happened? The student used the mechanism of the *Linking Mode* to retrieve prior knowledge of the sound of a waltz and then applied it to the performance.

Although I doubt that music teachers formally refer to this process as a third mode, they have traditionally been using third mode techniques for centuries to help young musicians develop mature interpretations of printed music. They sing to the student. They use metaphors. They reference the ability to make the music sound light and choppy like rain drops or even and flowing like rippling water.

In addition, music teachers often encourage their students to listen to more live music or quality recordings to increase their stored aural memory of many types of music.

Almost anyone who can read music can learn to access the third mode *if the teacher is skilled in teaching it*. Without this unique instruction, the notational reader only learns to play mechanically—decoding the music symbols on the staff, producing the correct tones on the instrument, reading rhythms, keeping the steady beat, and managing technical issues on the instrument—without ever feeling the joy of expressing meaning and emotion during the performance.

Examples from the Classroom

Musical expression should be introduced after the student masters all the technical elements required to perform a piece of music, and it should not be expected or required earlier than that. The long neural pathways for recognizing symbols (which are developed through many repetitions of exact information) must become stable and secure before adding a more complex process. Kinesthetic skills for operating the fingers on the instrument must also become so exact and accurate, over and over, that they become almost automatic. Then, and only then, can expressive elements be added without disturbing, distracting, or destroying any of the essential neural pathways for decoding and handling the instrument.

Throughout my teaching career, I've never seen one instance in which a student began reading standard notation in a musically meaningful way. Instead, students begin being totally consumed with visual reading issues and overcoming the difficulty of handling an adult-sized musical instrument. Over time, some students began to gradually be able to make the music come alive. But it never happened on its own; it was always the result of specific instruction.

There is no doubt in my mind that when it comes to developing the holistic aspects of instrumental music, students young and old have the ability to incorporate their inner feelings and musical expression as they read from the printed page. For years, I'd been calling this amazing ability the *art of reading music*.

Whether teaching students in their sixth week or the sixth year of instruction, I've encouraged them to stop and remember the way music really sounds. Under my guidance, many instrumental musicians have grown to deeply love the music they were playing. In return, hearing my students' interpretations and their unique ways of shaping and coloring their music has given me a tremendous amount of satisfaction as their teacher.

For years, I thought I was just teaching students to improve the expressive qualities of their music, but now I understand that I was really helping them use undeveloped *cognitive abilities*. Every time they accessed information from music memory through their third *Linking Mode* and applied it to their performance, their brain united their natural musical instincts with their technical, spatial, and kinesthetic abilities.

Conversely, I have also witnessed students reading music who, unfortunately, possessed no awareness of musical expression whatsoever. These students regarded excellence merely as the ability to play without pausing or the ability to "get through" the music without technical errors. In these cases, I would have to change teaching techniques. Instead of asking the student to remember the way the music should sound or just demonstrating how it should sound, I would describe mechanical ways to add expression: "Press the piano key longer (or stronger) for the first note of each measure." "Make the notes get louder in this measure, as if the sound is coming toward you." "Now make it softer as the music goes away from you." These comments act similarly to training wheels for learning to ride a bike. Once the student uses them long enough, they will be ready to play the music beautifully without prompting.

For me, both the presence of musical expression or lack thereof in instrumental music firmly establishes the theory that interpretive abilities are separate from spatial reading and qualify as a third mode.

When you read *Chapter 12: Tenets of Linking Mode*, you will see more examples from the classroom that will provide even further evidence that this third mode does, indeed, exist separately from *Aural* and *Notational Modes*.

Defining All Three Modes

When we combine *Aural, Notational,* and *Linking Modes,* every type of music cognition is explained. I believe these are the "plurality of mechanisms" that Gardner alluded to. I call them *The Three Modes of Music Cognition.*

The term "mode" means the manner in which something occurs or is experienced. Each mode in this three-mode model is based on a particular group of cognitive skills that operate a distinct set of tasks in the brain.

Aural Mode refers to our natural abilities in music guided by our auditory senses, our intuitive instincts about music, and our music intelligence.

Notational Mode refers to visual music activities and technical aspects of *decoding* printed music notation for vocal or instrumental performance guided by spatial and kinesthetic intelligences.

Linking Mode is a facilitator, accessing information from *Aural Mode* (stored memory of sounds that communicate meaning through music intelligence) to compare and refine music the performer is decoding in *Notational Mode*—in order to bring about aesthetic, holistic music.

Linking Mode and Professional Instrumentalists

The difference between the sounds of instrumental music played by beginning students and sounds produced by more mature musicians is the difference between using *Notational Mode* alone or elevating the performance into *Linking Mode* by adding musical expression.

Every professional instrumentalist, vocalist, and conductor who performs from printed music began in *Notational Mode* first and then acquired the cognitive skills for *Linking Mode.*

The good news for all of us involved in music education is that once we isolate and fully understand the tenets of Linking Mode, it becomes possible to teach the interpretive properties of music to *everyone*—not just those who are considered exceptionally talented.

Chapter 4

Steady Beat

In the upcoming chapters, we are going to be looking closely at the tenets of the three modes as they relate to music education. But before we do, it is important to acknowledge a *fourth* cognitive process in music that operates in the background of each of the three modes—steady beat, also known as steady pulse. Steady beat may be the most prominent feature of music—not only because it is always present, but because *the feel of the steady pulse instantly unites the performer and the audience.*

Three Types of Steady Beat Abilities in Each Mode

The *first type* of steady beat cognition is the ability to keep the beat steady. The brain knows and regulates the space between beats. We will discuss that ability later in this chapter in greater detail.

The *second type* of steady beat cognition is the ability to process beats in metered groups such as meter in 4 (Loud, soft, soft, soft) or meter in 3 (Loud, soft, soft). These repeated segments always begin with a loud beat followed by softer beats. This means the brain not only regulates the distance between each pulse but also regulates the pattern of loud and soft pulses.

The *third type* of steady beat cognition is the ability to always be aware of which beat in a measure is being used.

Students are taught early on to emphasize the first beat of a measure—which establishes the feeling of meter. For example, in a 4/4 piece of music, the beats in every measure would sound this way: "loud-soft-soft-soft." In 3/4 they would be "loud, soft, soft."

One of my favorite examples of how important it is to understand the role of individual beats is the way a rock drummer uses the fourth beat of every measure. If the drummer is spot on when he hits the fourth beat every time, the audience will really connect to the music. If the drummer is sloppy on the fourth beats, the sound of the band will be unappealing.

Our brain is capable of not only keeping a steady beat but staying aware of which beat is being used and the special ways of emphasizing each beat.

I believe the ability to emphasize certain beats more than others—as well as the fact that beats fluctuate in strength according to the intuitive whims of the performer—makes it very likely that the emphasis on certain beats is regulated by *music and personal intelligences*.

But the evenness of the basic beat is managed by *spatial intelligence*, as a feature of recognizing *distance* (between beats).

In addition, when the performer vocally or mentally numbers the beats while performing, saying, "one, two, three, four," in each 4/4 measure, the performer is using logical-math intelligence.

How the Musician Experiences Steady Beat

The brain treats steady beat a little differently depending on which music mode is in use.

In **Aural Mode**, when we sing a song, we make up our own beat and sing along with it. We are so accustomed to our own internal beat that it feels as if steady beat is just part of the song. This internal beat is part of our natural musical sense and is possibly acquired as music intelligence develops in early years.

On the other hand, when we express ourselves through dance or marching, instead of our own internal beat, we are reacting to an *external beat* (the audio source of the music). To do so, we must listen carefully in order to direct the muscles in our body to align with the sound of the steady beat we are listening to. This would be a combination of *music intelligence* and *kinesthetic intelligence* (and *spatial intelligence*, as I will show in a moment when we look at walking to a steady beat).

Children develop their awareness of steady beat through Aural Mode activities in elementary general music through fun songs that require nodding their heads, clapping their hands, patting their knees, etc. to the *sound* of the steady beat. Some children are hearing the beat of the music and reacting to it. But other children who haven't yet developed an aural sensitivity to the beat may actually be visually reacting to the motions of the teacher or other students in the room. Even copying others is an important first step in beat training because it trains kinesthetic intelligence to perform actions at regular intervals. Kinesthetic memory helps the child eventually be able to create an internal beat without assistance, and it may lead to the ability to hear the beat in the music without visual clues from others in the room.

In **Notational Mode**, steady beat is also experienced a number of ways:

- internally, as a self-directed activity when performing alone
- in response to the external beat of a metronome
- in response to the external beat of an audio source, such as the ensemble that the musician is performing in, recorded music, or vocal sounds from the instructor
- in response to the visual cues of the conductor's baton

In **Linking Mode**, steady beat is treated the same as in *Notational Mode*. The only difference is that Linking Mode is all about accessing and using musical expression. In Linking Mode, the performer's steady beat may quicken or slow to express a particular mood or feeling. These tempo changes do not alter the fact that the beat is steady. These changes are usually subtle or gradual enough to help the listener anticipate where each new beat will occur. Therefore, we still say this slightly altered beat is regular and steady.

Professional Standards for Steady Beat

How steady does the beat have to be? As a general rule, the closer a person gets to performing professionally, the more exacting the timing becomes. In other words, when small children "clap to the beat," they produce a beat that is approximate. Their claps may not be spaced apart in exact measurements. The more a person performs alone and with others, the more noticeable the beat becomes to the listeners and the greater the requirement for exactness.

During a summer break while I was a public-school band director, I took some guitar lessons from an old road musician named Howey who turned out to be a fantastic teacher. He insisted, however, that I go back to basics and tap my foot as I strummed and picked the guitar strings.

When he kept insisting, I became a little annoyed. I truly did not think I needed to go back to the basics. If I were a rank beginner, I would expect to be asked to tap my toe in order to learn to count properly, but I was far from a beginner—I was a band director. Surely I was keeping a very adequate steady beat, even without toe-tapping. Tapping my foot for Howey seemed unnecessary, even childish. I preferred to just move my shoulders and upper body slightly to the beat.

However, Howey was adamant. He refused to accept my excuses. It soon became apparent that we would have to do it his way if he and I were going to play songs together in my lesson.

I have to admit—he was right. There was surprising room for improvement, and I noticed the difference.

Here are three important lessons I learned from Howey:

- We are never too educated to learn something new.
- We can't scoff at the basics—they really work!

- It's very possible that toe-tapping sends a stronger signal to the brain for measuring the steady beat than using more subtle demonstrations such as nodding or moving our shoulders. When our foot shows the downbeat and upbeat of every beat, all beats become perfectly equal, every time.

Steady Beat for School Children

Research and educational practices as far back as the 1970s have shown that children's ability to demonstrate steady beat reveals their level of whole-body coordination. And that, in turn, is linked to their cognitive development.

My first introduction to the concept of *children's body coordination* occurred when I was working as a teacher for a private organization called The Children's Health Program in Great Barrington, Massachusetts in conjunction with Boston Medical Center. I was in charge of three to four playgroups that met each week for mothers, infants, and toddlers. Then, every Friday, we playgroup teachers joined the medical staff discussing case studies involving pre-school children in our local area with physical or learning disabilities.

Through those staff meetings in the 1970s, I became a trained resource for families for the health and wellness of their children. I supported mothers' concerns about their children's growth and behaviors, referring families to our medical staff when needed.

I was trained to notice areas in child development that might warrant helpful intervention. One of those areas was the importance of toddlers being able to crawl. In our staff meetings, we discussed how children who skipped crawling, going straight from creeping to standing to walking, were more likely to have difficulties later in school with learning to read. It became part of my job to see that the children-and-mothers play groups I directed included plenty of crawling activities in addition to music, art, and nutrition.

In writing this book, I was unable to find any research that conclusively linked crawling to reading abilities. However, I can personally attest to the topic of crawling being anecdotally discussed and implemented in the 1970s as a remedial approach for extreme reading difficulties (in the Massachusetts area). Children in first and second grades with reading difficulties who had never learned to crawl were shown how to get down on the floor and crawl. Supposedly, this coordination of the right and left side of their bodies improved their abilities in reading.

While the cognitive benefits of crawling were never conclusively proven, other research about left and right body coordination was taking place in Michigan in the 1970s, which went on to produce measurable results.

Research in Steady Beat Abilities

During the 1970s (and unknown to me at the time), a physical education teacher and researchist from the High Scope Institute, Ypsilanti, Michigan, **Phyllis J. Weikart (1931-2016)**, had begun evaluating steady beat coordination in children. Her work showed that children in the 1970s were less able to walk to a steady beat than years prior. Her research for several decades (1970s through 1990s) showed a continuing decline in children's steady beat skills along with a corresponding decline in their standardized test scores in reading, math, and spelling.

> **Special note to teachers who do not believe in using standardized tests:** While it is true that standardized tests have led to negative practices in education such as "teaching to the test" or penalizing schools based on test scores, none of that happened in the Weikart studies.
>
> Weikart created her own assessment tools for measuring children's body coordination. Then, to complete the comparison with academics, she used scores for standardized tests in math, spelling, and reading—which are still the most reliable academic assessment tools we have to compare cognitive abilities with body coordination.

Weikart attributed the decline in steady beat abilities to American cultural changes in childrearing practices such as less rocking of babies at birth, less patting of babies to steady beat (parents using rhythmic patting of song words instead), and keeping children inside the home more (with fewer playground games that develop beat, such as hopscotch and jump rope).

The Criteria for Whole Body Coordination

Weikart measured steady beat abilities in *weightbearing* muscles. She *did not* measure sedentary clapping (while the child is seated). Instead, her research was about *whole-body* movement that depended on applying body weight to the feet. One of her standard measurements for whole body coordination was the ability to accurately walk forward, then backward, at least eight successive steps to an audio source, such as march music.

Notice that crawling is also a weightbearing activity wherein the child's full weight is on the knees and forearms. In crawling, the right forearm is forward when the left knee is forward. Conversely, the left forearm moves with the right knee. In other words, the child who is crawling is coordinating muscles on opposite sides of the body. This is sometimes referred to as cross-body coordination. Further on in this chapter, you will see that Weikart put a lot of emphasis on cross-body coordination in observing how the feet should move opposite to the swinging of the arms while walking.

How the Brain Regulates Steady Beat

While kinesthetic intelligence *moves* the muscles, spatial intelligence decides *how often* and *how far* to move the muscles. How does the brain use spatial intelligence to do that?

Spatial intelligence includes our sense of where things are located around us, such as how far we are sitting from an exit, how far others are situated from us in a room, or in the world. A person who is blind learns the location of objects in their home and workplace through spatial intelligence.

However, spatial intelligence is not limited to the location of physical objects.

If we can *sense* where objects are, we can also *sense points in time*. When the "object in space" is a point in time, we learn to sense the distance from one point in time to another. As a result, we learn the timed distance of a second, a minute, a half-hour, an hour. Some of us are able to wake up at the same time every morning because we sense the distance in time—either from when we went to bed or from that exact waking moment the previous day. Personally, I am able to take a "power nap" of three minutes, five minutes, or twenty minutes, depending on the directions I give myself for waking up.

If spatial intelligence gives us the ability to know *distances in time*, it also gives us the ability to calculate the distance between one beat and the next. And it helps us regulate equal distances between beats. This means that people who have trouble keeping a steady beat may be lacking in the spatial perception for timed distances.

If a person lacks ability to keep a steady beat, the teacher can create a situation where the person will learn to regulate the distance between beats by having the person swing their arms to and fro as they walk or march. This swinging-arm-motion helps *time the distances* between footsteps. Upper- and lower-body motion results in a better sense of beat than just using the legs, reinforcing the idea that whole-body coordination produces a more *accurate* steady beat (rather than just hand-clapping or marching).

This is how whole-body coordination works. Picture a pendulum set into motion, swinging back and forth evenly through gravitational force. That's how our arms behave when we walk with total body coordination—our arms swing in the opposite direction of our walking steps. We feel the equally timed swing of our arms and how long that swing takes. We coordinate our feet with our arms. When we decide to walk faster, we think we are just directing our feet, but we may actually be directing the pendulum motion of our arms first, which in turn directs the timing of the feet.

Without the pendulous swinging of the arms, which serve as a built-in mechanism for walking evenly, a steady beat is much more difficult to achieve. In the Weikart method of remediation for steady-beat deficiencies, the teacher surveys children as they walk, taking particular notice of those children whose upper bodies appear "frozen." This is a sign that their whole-body coordination is not yet established.

Other Uses For Steady Beat

In addition to our ability to walk, dance, or perform music to a steady beat, our brain has the cognitive ability to create a steady beat separately in our mind before we begin playing a song or pattern—even when our body is not moving at all—because we can "think the beat." We can verbally add a "count-off" measure ahead of beginning the music, such as saying, "One, two, ready, play."

Likewise, when we listen to music, spatial recognition helps us isolate the beat and differentiate it from rhythm patterns in the music. It also helps us notice irregularities when the beat falters or changes.

Connecting Steady Beat to Cognitive Development

While Weikart's research pointed out a *decline* in steady beat abilities, I would like to speak about something different—how cognitive skills may *increase* by improving steady beat skills and whole-body coordination.

During the 1990s, I met Phyllis Weikart for the first time when I attended one of her workshops near Tampa, Florida. I was so impressed with her methods that I ordered all of her teaching manuals and folkdance recordings for my elementary music curriculum at Citrus Springs Elementary School in Citrus Springs, Florida.

For the next year, I tested steady beat accuracy in students of every grade level, K-5. While using the Weikart games and folk dances, I tested students again and again. Our students at Citrus Springs Elementary at first reflected the same percentages of body coordination per class as Weikart's research had indicated—that seventy percent of students in each class could walk to the beat. Then, using her remedial methods, I was able to raise those scores.

Sometimes, when the first and second grade teachers arrived at my music room to pick up their students from music, the students would be finishing one of the Weikart folk dances. I would encourage the teachers to peek in the doorway and watch the feet of their students. The teachers were amazed that students who were not stepping accurately to the music were often the at-risk students in math or reading. They were even more amazed to watch these students improve in both body coordination and academic abilities over months of participation in the Weikart strategies.

However, the most positive feedback I received that year came from the Title I teachers who routinely administered a pull-out program to assist children with reading difficulties.

One afternoon near the end of the school year, two of the Chapter One teachers came to my classroom. They told me how they were in a quandary as to why Citrus Springs students were showing an unusual spike in reading improvement for that school year. Through a process of elimination, they had chosen my music program as the most influential factor in improving reading abilities schoolwide. They wanted to know what I was doing and how I was doing it. I showed them the Weikart materials and my testing results for steady beat abilities.

And then, there is also the story of Mitch, a fourth-grade boy at Citrus Springs Elementary who had begun piano lessons the previous September. At first, he had such an undeveloped sense of timing that he was unable to accurately measure or demonstrate half notes and whole notes, which I found to be very unusual for his age. It was obvious to me that the actions of his fingers on the piano keys had no cognitive connection to regular pulses of any kind. One day I asked him to stand up and move to the center of the room. I tested his ability to walk to a steady beat, the same as I had tested countless others in general music. His footsteps did not match the beat of the music at all. Over the next few months, we spent a few minutes each week in lessons helping him practice stepping to the steady beat. And he did improve.

The remarkable part of this story came at the end of the school year when I suggested to his mother that we take some weeks off in the summer to come back ready and refreshed in the fall. She was in sharp disagreement with my decision. "He's just gotten on the right track, and now you want to stop for a while!"

She went on to explain that Mitch had so many problems reading that he had been placed in Chapter One classes at the beginning of that school year. However, since taking piano lessons, he improved in reading so much that he no longer qualified for those services. She believed that reading music in piano lessons was the key factor in her son's academic improvement.

I believe his academic reading progressed from the combination of two things—learning better eye motion techniques in reading notation and moving his body to the sound of the steady beat.

Methods that Develop Large Motor Responses to Music

Here are some special methodologies that train spatial and kinesthetic responses to music:

- **Phyllis S. Weikart's** (1931-2016) recordings and books for the music classroom such as *Teaching Movement & Dance: A Sequential Approach to Rhythmic Movement*. And *Round the Circle: Key Experiences in Movement for Young Children* (High/Scope Press).

- Eurythmics method by **Emile Jaques-Dalcroze** (1865-1950), a Swiss composer and educator who developed whole body movements to sense, interpret, and express the nuances and aesthetic meaning of the music. For more information, contact: Dalcroze Society of America at www.dalcrozeusa.org.

Steady Beat and the Three Modes

Because the beat is so simple, compared to interesting rhythm patterns, and because it is regular and often feels so automatic, we may often take steady beat for granted. We don't realize that the brain is purposefully regulating the spaces between beats. Nor have we realized how essential steady beat is for the development of body coordination and the whole brain.

Even though steady beat abilities are not front and center in the production of music, steady beat is always present. It is as important to music as tracks are to a train. The beat is the foundation of all the music produced in the three modes. And that means the spatial intelligence skills of steady beat are always operating in the background in addition to the cognitive abilities within each of the three modes.

When a student reads music during home practice for thirty minutes, I would estimate that twenty of those minutes are spent drilling and improving the neural pathways for many intelligences at once. For a sixty-minute band or orchestra rehearsal, at least forty minutes would require students to not only operate within their own performance capacity but coordinate their timing, volume, and musical expression with others in the ensemble.

Is there any other subject in the school curriculum that trains children to use their brains this fully and on a daily basis?

As we discover the cognitive process within each mode, you will more fully understand the role of music in helping children learn to process information, especially if we keep in mind that music activities always include steady beat skills, as well.

Chapter 5

Tenets of Aural Mode

The first music mode we experience in life is Aural Mode. Similar to the way we learn to understand language, we also learn to associate musical sounds and sound patterns with meaning and communication. These skills emerge so early that part of the Suzuki instrumental program requires expectant parents to play recordings of classical music for their children *before birth* while still in the womb. These pre-birth experiences are a preparation for Suzuki violin training later when the child can stand and walk.

Aural Mode is experienced auditorily—through hearing, creating, and organizing sound. It is also experienced intuitively, giving us the abilities used to describe, evaluate, and compare music.

Brief Outline of Aural Mode

The following list shows basic music skills in Aural Mode that I compiled by referencing the 2014 Music Standards for PreK-8 General Music Standards provided by the National Association for Music Education. (You can find these standards at **nafame.org/my-classroom/standards/core-music-standards**). In a moment, you will see a list of music skills I associate with aural mode. Next to each skill, you will see coded letters that indicate which of Gardner's intelligences have the *greatest* influence and benefit.

It's important to note that the three intelligences most prevalent are:

- **Music intelligence** (the ability to recognize and vocalize pitches and rhythms; to demonstrate "perfect" or "relative" pitch; to listen to music and remember it; and to compose music.)
- **Personal intelligence** (the ability to make choices about music; attach meaning to music; and develop preferences for certain activities or songs over others.)
- **Kinesthetic intelligence** (the ability to direct motor skills and physical coordination for clapping, dancing, and playing instruments.)

Table of Codes for Intelligences
K=Kinesthetic, **L**=Language, **LM**=Logical-Math
M=Music, **P**=Personal,
SP-r =Spatial Recognition, **SP-t** = Spatial Transformation

Tasks Within Aural Mode

Creating sound
Singing **(M, P, L)**
Clapping **(M, K)**
Vocally imitating sounds **(M, SP-r)**
Making sounds using found objects **(M, P, K)**
Making sounds using musical instruments **(M, P, K)**

Exploring sound
Experimenting with high and low sounds **(M)**
Experimenting with timbres, dynamics, tempos **(M, P)**
Experimenting with rhythm, **(M, L, SP-r, P)**
Experimenting with language patterns **(M, L, SP-r, P)**
Improvising, playing "by ear" **(M, SP-r, P, K)**

Examining Sound
Listening to various styles, multicultural **(M)**
Critiquing, describing music **(M, P, L)**

Organizing Sound (Composing)
Making up short sound patterns **(M, P)**
Connecting short patterns **(M, P)**
Understanding musical form **(M, L, SP-r)**
Transposing, Modulating **(M, SP-r, SP-t)**

Intelligences Needed for Aural Mode

As you can see from that list, *music intelligence* is the chief guiding factor in Aural Mode in everything from singing to the use of sound patterns, improvising, listening to music, and analyzing it. These activities train a child's auditory skills so they can differentiate nuances in timbre, the repetition of sounds, and pitch differences. Music intelligence is where we get our holistic sense of music and the ability to be expressive through music.

The second most important is *personal intelligence*, which helps us formulate decisions and personal choices about music.

Music intelligence and personal intelligence work hand in hand. While music intelligence helps us recognize pitches and patterns of sounds, personal intelligence helps us create our own unique expression through music. When used together, we are able to communicate feelings and ideas through musical sounds.

General music classes in school help children develop many of the following cognitive processes for Aural Mode:

- *Responding to music*
- *Creating, demonstrating, and organizing musical ideas*

- *Improvising patterns of sound*
- *Generating simple phrases*
- *Interpreting and evaluating music*
- *Demonstrating knowledge of concepts*
- *Analyzing selected music*
- *Performing music*

In music class, the activities that develop these abilities are singing and improvising on pitched and non-pitched percussion instruments, as well as listening to many live and recorded examples of music.

When these aural experiences are stored in permanent memory, they serve as musical road maps later for improvising and creating more music that is meaningful and expressive.

Requirements for Conformity in Aural Mode

Most skills in Aural Mode, such as imitating and creating music, are developed through exploration. However, there are two skills in Aural Mode that do require conformity to strict standards. One is *singing on pitch* and the other is *keeping a steady beat*. A devoted and conscientious teacher will pay a great deal of attention and time helping each student develop these two important aspects of musicianship. Let me explain why.

Singing "On-pitch?"

Singing "on pitch" is also called singing "in tune." In some cultures, the overall sound of a multitude of voices singing together is expected to sound "thick" due to voices being similar in frequency but not perfectly matched. However, attitudes toward matching pitches within most Western cultures are exactly the opposite. We expect a group of voices to perfectly match in frequency and therefore produce a "thin" unified sound.

In American culture, we say an individual either sings *in tune* or *out of tune*. There is no area in between. This is similar to *being on time* or *arriving late*. A person can only do one or the other—there is no alternative middle ground. In music, the cycles per second of two tones either match or do not.

Another way of saying it is that the two sources of sound *come into agreement*. Numerically and scientifically, if one source vibrates at 436 cycles per second and the second source vibrates at 440 cycles per second, they are not in agreement.

It is impractical to attempt to achieve perfect agreement of pitches in an elementary music classroom with twenty or more students. In general music classes, we do not use scientific equipment to measure the pitch accuracy of children's voices; instead, teachers listen. They evaluate whether a student's voice sounds as if it is generally matching the pitches of other students or the pitches of the piano. The ideal we would like to achieve, but seldom can, is for the frequency of two pitches to come into complete agreement so that it's difficult to hear they are from different sound sources.

By using fun games such as vocally making siren sounds and animal sounds, children are encouraged to expand their vocal range from one or two tones to five, eight, or more. Similarly, by engaging in imitation games with the teacher and each other, students learn to make their voice match other tones. This takes time and patience. Eventually, it is hoped that children will acquire the same keen evaluation of pitch agreement possessed by the teacher.

When a child is taught to hear pitches and regulate their own voice to match tones of an instrument or of other singers, these newly acquired skills actually improve the child's self-esteem and opinion of themselves. The child goes from saying "I can't sing" to "I can sing." Most people carry the label of being able to sing (or not) with them throughout their lifetime. For this reason, intervening early to help a child in elementary school conform to a high standard for matching pitches is a very worthwhile endeavor.

More About Formal Pitch Training

Some of the special pitch programs and the music educators who developed them include:

Solfege, a system of giving each tone in the scale a syllable name such as "Do, Re Mi, etc." These are also called *solmization syllables*. Early Chinese, Indian, Greek, and Byzantine cultures used syllables for tones. The first written evidence of solfege syllables is from the 11th century associated with Guido of Arezzo.

Zoltán Kodály (1882-1967), Hungarian composer credited with the development of music education in Hungary, taught musical literacy by teaching children to sing through solfege. He developed hand signs for each degree of the scale that became popular in general music classes in our country. For more information about Kodály methods, contact: www.oake.org for the Organization of American Kodály Education or www.iks.hu for the International Kodály Society.

Carl Orff (1895-1982), German conductor, composer, and music educator who collaborated with music educators **Dorothee Gunther** (1896-1975) and **Gunild Keetman** (1904-1990). They developed music education that combined art, dance, music, language, and theater. Their aim was to find the "existing rhythm within." A singing exercise in this method uses solfege syllables in a vertical list, visible to the class, to teach new songs. The teacher points to syllables in the vertical list, leading the children through short rote sections of a song until they learn it. Large wooden Orff xylophones have become standard equipment in general music classrooms in the U.S. for children to experiment with pitch and rhythm patterns in the Orff-Schulwerk method. For more information, contact: www.aosa.org at American Orff-Schulwerk Association.

Shinichi Suzuki (1898-1998), Japanese violinist, conductor, and educator. He helped children develop exceptional abilities in performance by teaching them to play an instrument the way they learned language—by listening and imitating. In the Suzuki Method, music is learned through the auditory senses (through music intelligence) and transferred to the instrument (through spatial transformation). Students develop advanced performance skills auditorily before learning to read notation. For more information, contact: www.suzukiassociation.org for Suzuki Association of the Americas.

Chapter 6

Tenets of Notational Mode

As you begin this chapter, notice how different the tenets of Notational Mode are from Aural Mode. Here in Notational Mode, there is an absence of words such as "holistic, meaningful music" because now the priority is *technical abilities* guided by *spatial and kinesthetic intelligences*.

This doesn't mean that the person who studies a musical instrument is destined or doomed to play music void of meaning and beauty. It just means that notational abilities are the first step—the technical step—which is refined at the appropriate time later by adding musical expression through *Linking Mode*.

Until the student can accurately read music notation, produce characteristic tone on the instrument, and completely control the sound coming from the instrument, no amount of musical expression will please an audience. All the audience will notice in a technically poor performance is the pauses, the speeding up in easy parts and slowing down in difficult parts, the wrong notes, or the poor tone quality. Until a student has "ironed out" all errors in a song—in any song, be it simple or difficult—the student's efforts to be expressive will be premature and wasted. That's why technique is mastered first.

Most instrumental teachers know it's risky to bring up the subject of musical expression when the student is still struggling with technical accuracy. When just starting out, students can easily resent too many simultaneous directives and grow to feel that the teacher is never satisfied, no matter what the student fixes or how hard they try. But once technique is mastered and the student feels more relaxed, musical expression and interpretive skills can more successfully be introduced—even on songs as simple as "Twinkle, Twinkle, Little Star."

Brief Outline of Notational Mode

Notational Mode is experienced visually through a complex set of rules governing music notation. It is also experienced kinesthetically as the performer trains parts of the body to operate the musical instrument.

Notational Mode occurs at three different levels during the reading process. If we are to offer remedial help to students quickly, we must first be able to identify at which of these levels the error occurred:

1) Reading information on the page

2) Transferring the information from page to instrument

3) Operating the instrument to match the notation on the page of music.

Next, you'll find a list of forty-two skills for *Notational Mode* that have been garnered from my own teaching experience. Unlike the aural skills, these could not be taken from the national music goals because our national goals do not contain specific benchmarks for reading music in grades PreK through eighth grade. (For more information about the national goals, see **Addendum 2:** *The National Music Goals in Relation to Reading Music.*)

Each of the forty-two skills include coded letters for the intelligences most involved. Again, it is not my intention to exclude the presence of other intelligences or other factors but merely to point out which intelligences I believe have the *greatest* influence and benefit in processing musical notation.

You'll notice the *overwhelming* influence of spatial and kinesthetic intelligences. Here is a reminder of what these intelligences mean:

- **Spatial Recognition** (the ability to recognize objects in space according to shape, distance, or direction—visually deciphering notation)

- **Spatial Transformation** (the ability to transfer knowledge from one system to another system without losing the meaning of the information)

- **Kinesthetic intelligence** (the ability to monitor and direct motor skills and physical coordination needed for pressing keys, finding frets, covering finger holes, operating valves and slides, forming embouchure and hand positions)

> In my view, there are few other subjects in the school curriculum that develop spatial intelligence to this degree. Notational Mode includes many visual and transformation skills required for the student to read notes, operate the instrument, and coordinate every sound with steady beat—but the most amazing part of notational reading is that many of these skills operate simultaneously.

Table of Codes for Intelligences
K=Kinesthetic, **L**=Language, **LM**=Logical-Math
M=Music, **P**=Personal,
SP-r =Spatial Recognition, **SP-t** = Spatial Transformation

Tasks Within Notational Mode

Recognition of Shapes on the Music Staff
Shapes of rhythmic symbols (quarter note, etc.) **(SP-r)**
Shapes of clef signs, time and key signatures **(SP-r)**
Shapes of measures, bar lines **(SP-r)**
Position of a note head in relation to lines of the staff **(SP-r)**
Shapes of beams, flags, rests, dots, slurs, ties **(SP-r)**
Shapes of melodic lines that run parallel or contrary **(SP-r)**

Difference between *step-wise* and larger intervals **(SP-r)**
Recognizing notes going line-line-line or space-space-space **(SP-r)**
Recognizing notes on, above, or below ledger lines **(SP-r)**

Recognition of Shapes on the Staff written for Keyboard, Harp, or Guitar
The shape of multiple note heads on one stem **(SP-r)**
The shape of line-triads and space-triads **(SP-r)**
The shape of an inverted chord **(SP-r)**

Recognition of Direction on the Music Staff
Note heads that are ascending; descending. **(SP-r)**
The exact point at which note heads reverse direction **(SP-r)**

Recognition of Distance on the Music Staff
Noticing distances that go line to line, space to space **(SP-r)**
Noticing leaps of seconds, thirds, fourths, etc. **(SP-r)**
Recognizing in which octave the notes occur **(SP-r)**

Associating Alphabet Names with Shapes on the Music Staff
Understanding alphabet runs vertically upward **(SP-r, SP-t)**
Understanding every line and space receive a letter **(SP-t)**
Understanding the alphabet in ledger line areas **(SP-r, SP-t)**

Understanding and Utilizing Rhythmic Concepts
Duration **(LM, SP-r, SP-t)**
Rhythmic patterns **(SP-r, M)**
Meter and time signatures **(LM, SP-t)**
Compound and simple time **(LM, SP-t)**
Incomplete measures **(LM, SP-t)**
Divisions of the beat **(LM, SP-r, SP-t)**
Ties **(LM, SP-r, SP-t)**

Understanding and Utilizing Harmonic Concepts
Scale, positions in the scale **(SP-t)**
Fundamental chord structure **(SP-t)**

Harmonic and melodic intervals **(SP-t)**
Modulation, transposition **(SP-t)**

Producing the Instrument's Characteristic Tone
Body posture and proper breathing **(K)**
Embouchure, for brasses and woodwinds **(K)**
Finger or bow pressure for string instruments **(K)**
Appropriate curved finger shape and pressure **(K, SP-r)**
Using live or recorded examples of tone as a model **(M, P)**

Learning Finger Positions Along with Assigned Alphabet Labels
Learning shapes of the finger or slide positions **(K, SP-r)**
Learning the alphabet name of each slide position, string position, key, or finger combination **(L, SP-r)**
Visualizing the whole alphabet on horn, keyboard, or string instrument **(SP-t)**

Transformation of Staff Information to Instrument Positions
Matching alphabet on the staff to corresponding alphabet designations on the instrument **(SP-t)**
Matching the distance and direction on the staff with distance and direction on the instrument **(SP-t)**
Matching the octave area indicated on the staff with the proper octave on the instrument **(SP-t)**
Matching shapes on the staff with articulation on the instrument, for tonguing or finger-hand motion **(SP-t, K)**

> **Note to the Reader:** You may be unfamiliar with some of these skill descriptions. The skills and codes make sense to me because I work with these terms every day, both as a writer and teacher. However, they may be brand new to you. Because of that, some of you may have even chosen to scan the list quickly rather than read each individual item, thinking this section was too technical to be of interest. I fully understand. However, I would encourage you to come back to this section later after you finish all the tenets of Notational Mode in Chapters 7-11, at which point you'll hopefully be better prepared to fully absorb the rich magnitude of skills and cognitive benefits that emanate from this one single area of music education.

Research of Spatial and Kinesthetic Neurons

Even with a quick scan of the items in the *Notational Mode* outline, it should be evident that reading music predominantly uses spatial and kinesthetic intelligences—two areas of cognition that have recently become the focus of studies in neuroscience.

In 2017, Linda Overstreet-Wadiche and Jacques Wadiche from the Department of Neurobiology, University of Alabama, Birmingham, published a study entitled "Adult-born Neurons Modify Excitatory Synaptic Transmission." Scientists found neurogenesis in both the hippocampus and cerebellum, the regions for spatial and kinesthetic intelligence. They stated *moderate to vigorous physical activity* (MVPA) is the best way to stimulate the formation of new brain cells in those regions. As of this writing, they are also studying the effects of aerobic exercises on neurogenesis in spatial and kinesthetic intelligence.

Based on all the incidences of spatial and kinesthetic intelligence skills in *Notational Mode*, I suggest that scientists also look for neurogenesis as a person reads music and transfers the information to a musical instrument.

The fact that this study uses *moderate to vigorous physical activity* (MVPA) in order to build new brain cells suggests that we now have neurological evidence for requiring daily practice in order to learn how to read music and master the use of a musical instrument. As discussed before, neural pathways for these spatial and kinesthetic activities are not fully developed at birth and don't emerge on their own. So daily instrumental music practice may nudge and encourage the formation of new neural pathways—or greatly reconfigure old ones.

To the contrary, scientists in this particular study also reported that older, worn-out brain cells in the cerebral cortex transferred their synapses to new cells—*and less fit, older neurons faded away*. Again, this explains why students who slack off in regular daily practice seem to lose their momentum and sometimes become confused, frustrated, and less motivated.

Is this redistribution of synapses simply the way our brain stays vital? Or is it an indication that some activities can potentially go beyond mere cell maintenance to actually *increase* the brain's capabilities?

If we conclude that regular practice in reading music improves spatial reasoning and kinesthetic abilities, we may be closer to understanding why it improves standardized test scores in reading, math, and spelling. Afterall, academics and music reading share many of the same spatial and visual abilities for recognizing shapes, distance, and direction.

Spatial Skills begin in PreK

If we provide a broad music curriculum in elementary school that fully prepares students for a lifetime of music participation, it makes sense to begin that music program in PreK and kindergarten when students are already learning similar skills for academics.

The pre-reading skills developed in PreK and kindergarten for English literacy, such as recognizing geometric shapes, letters, and numbers, require the same eye movements and spatial intelligence skills children need for recognizing note shapes in music. The question arises, then—why do we teach one and not the other? Why have we omitted pre-reading exercises for standard music notation in early grades?

Furthermore, in the academic classroom, when students learn that a shape is called a "circle" or "square," they are developing language skills as well as their ability to understand and name symbols. Symbolism is a higher order (abstract) area of cognition. Wouldn't it enhance every student's higher order thinking ability if they learned to label both geometric *and* notational shapes during the first years in school? This would *double the amount of time* students spent on both spatial intelligence skills and higher order thinking skills.

Comprehensive Note Reading in Early Grades

Before I lay out the tenets of *Notational Mode*, I want to dispel the notion that notational reading in elementary grades is too time consuming, too difficult, or in any way inappropriate to implement in lower elementary grades.

In a perfect world, reading music would be taught along with academic reading-readiness activities such as recognizing alphabet letters and numbers. General music classes could further enhance children's eye-hand coordination by teaching children to read simple notation for student xylophones. Learning to strike the correct bars on the xylophone with mallets would correspond to similar academic *eye-hand coordination* activities like using scissors to cut and paste, doing puzzles, and learning to use a pencil to draw shapes, letters, and numbers—all prerequisites for reading and writing words.

In later grades, students in general music would further develop their spatial abilities by reading music for soprano recorders and then electronic keyboards. Students would learn the lower part of the music staff for a couple of years, then the middle, then the upper staff—in a systematic year-by-year program to build confidence and mastery. Children could be tested and given remedial help if they needed it, using similar accountability standards as those in the academic classroom.

To match these note-reading goals, publishers could modify general music books to include songs and music at the note-reading level appropriate for each grade. Then, when children sing in general music class, the books would reinforce staff reading, instead of the situation we have now in general music—no reading from the music staff. In most music classrooms today, students may enjoy the pictures in the general music books and mimic the sound of their teacher's voice (or the pre-recorded music), but they are unable to read the notation the publisher has provided for each song. Why? Because few elementary students read music notation!

Would a comprehensive music reading program take up too much general music time? Not necessarily. The entire program could be *integrated* into short ten- or twenty-minute segments so there would still be adequate time for all aspects of creating, listening to, and evaluating music. (For a more in-depth description of this type of five-year music curriculum, see Chapter 15: Effective Notational Reading Programs.)

Under this plan, third grade students would have acquired enough working knowledge of the music staff to be able to perform from scores and compose written compositions. Third and fourth graders would be better prepared to make choices about music electives such as band or orchestra because they would have already experienced reading notation for a musical instrument. And all students would acquire excellent spatial and kinesthetic skills that would further enhance their learning in the academic classroom.

Major Considerations in Notational Mode

Learning to read music notation is a multi-layered system of skills involving rhythm, timing, pitch, and technical ability on the musical instrument. Simple aspects of *Notational Mode* can be learned slowly, year by year, in general music classes. More complex knowledge can be acquired through ensembles and private lessons, both of which require daily instrumental or vocal practice.

Regardless of the speed or intensity of the music instruction, most tenets of *Notational Mode* are best learned in a particular order as skills are mastered at one level before proceeding to the next. Once a student understands one element, the student is ready to learn the next, more complex element.

How Does the Teacher Learn the Order of Skills?

Instrumental teaching-methods classes at the college or university level are designed to sharpen a young music teacher's *classroom management* and *program development*. But knowing *what to teach* begins long before the instrumentalist reaches higher education. It begins the moment that person picks up their first musical instrument, attends their first music lesson, and joins their first ensemble. By engaging in ten or more years of hands-on reading and performing before becoming a teacher, he or she has time to develop a deep, intuitive awareness of what must be taught first, then second, then third, etc. Through repeated failures and recoveries, the musician experiences which kind of foundational knowledge will hold up and which will crumble. Young teachers know what to teach when they have run the gauntlet themselves and won the prize—professional musicianship.

An easier answer to the question of how the teacher learns the proper order is simply that they follow the order presented in a good lesson book series. And if something seems missing, the teacher will supplement either with a different lesson book or with materials the teacher creates such as flash cards or technical exercises.

Conversely, music education majors, who may or may not have experienced that kind of rigorous mastery in reading music for an instrument, may view the *order of skills* as less important. I can't emphasize the following point enough. If a music major who disavows the order of skills ultimately becomes a music teacher, their unrealistic point of view can adversely affect the way they teach reading music in the general music classroom. It can affect the methods they use, the age level at which they introduce notation, and how much time they choose to give it in the classroom.

A person who has climbed the steepest hill will know more about the pitfalls and shortcuts of climbing than someone who has never climbed at all. Similarly, the teacher who has overcome multiple obstacles in note-reading is more likely to pay attention to the small steps necessary in the reading process than someone with less experience. They are far *less likely* to experiment with methods that teach children to mimic reading (as a learned response or memorized action) and far *more likely* to require children to understand each and every pre-requisite step leading up to any new knowledge.

The good news is that any teacher can learn the order of skills and concepts in *Notational Mode*, regardless of previous music training by reading the following chapters that contain many clues about order and why it is necessary.

Has anyone ever catalogued or listed the steps required in reading music? Or, for that matter, explained why *the order* of these steps is so important?

It seems to me that a written document on this topic would give all of us a starting point, a platform, from which to add or delete. It would also reveal the rationale behind the decisions we make in our schools about reading music.

To that end, the following five chapters are devoted to an in-depth discussion of our system of reading music from the music staff—exposing the hidden rules we take for granted so they can be successfully passed on to any average learner. We might think of these next chapters as a condensed version of the body of knowledge I mentioned a moment ago—the knowledge the young instrumentalist experiences and intuitively learns through eight, ten, or twelve years of music training. In other words, it's the knowledge that forms the basis for effective instruction in reading music.

Along the way, we'll also discuss information that most teachers *are not* aware of. Recent neurological studies have been conducted with a direct bearing on music. I will also share my new strategies for *introducing notational reading early* and for *diagnosing note-reading difficulties.*

The following chapters explain Notational Mode in detail:

- (Chapter 7) Hierarchy in Notational Mode
- (Chapter 8) Abstraction and Symbolism
- (Chapter 9) The Importance of Process
- (Chapter 10) Training the Eyes
- (Chapter 11) Alphabetic Logic

Keep in mind that these tenets form the foundation of *decoding* music notation. Then Linking Mode adds to this foundation later by introducing musical expression—whether the student is playing a simple nursery rhyme melody or learning a three-page performance solo.

Chapter 7

Hierarchy in Notational Mode

In general, the word "hierarchy" refers to an arrangement of information according to size, shape, time, cost, or ability—from great to small, more to less, and vice versa.

Hierarchy allows us to file information in permanent memory, in logical order, usually from simple to complex.

A common example of hierarchy in education can be found in the way we teach numbers—not just at school but also at home. For a child, numbers are never introduced using the number three or higher. Instead, the first number they learn is the number one followed by the number two: "You may have one cookie." "I will ask you to do that one more time." "Show me one finger. Show me two."

When information is filed according to hierarchy, it is easier to retrieve and implement.

In formal education, the litmus test for whether or not we teach information in hierarchical order is student behavior. If students use the information better when they learn it in hierarchical order, then we know for sure that we've used the correct process.

Therefore, we should not put children through processes we simply *believe* are hierarchical unless we can justify them with *measurable student progress*.

I mention this because not all hierarchical learning is practical or useful; this is particularly true when it comes to teaching music. (For more information on this topic, see **Addendum 3:** *Aural Myths in General Music*.)

Operational Hierarchy in Standard Notation

In Notational Mode, a student's knowledge of rhythm, timing, and duration has to be acquired in a particular hierarchical order of simple to complex so that this knowledge is *stable*.

Stable means:

1. The information is not just memorized but acquired through repeated practice and use (the process of building the long neural pathways). Therefore, this knowledge makes so much sense and becomes so useful that it will not completely disappear if the student takes time off from learning for vacation time, an illness, or moving to another school. Conversely, memorized information that is in random order, that does not make logical sense, can fade away *without use and practice*.

2. When the information is learned during childhood, it's learned *in a form* that is still applicable and *useful later as an adult musician*. (Unlike temporary methods like learning to play music through a coded color system.) This element of stability is what was meant by "college and career readiness," the exact phrase used on the Common Core State Initiative website: **http://www.corestandards.org/about-the-standards/development-process/.**

3. The information is introduced as *simple concepts* that are so easy to understand that the student can rearrange the information to use it in a variety of ways and not restricted to fixed, memorized, pre-designed patterns.

The instrumental teacher's goal is to empower the student to read music independently, which means learning to sight-read a new piece of music, interpret it, and perform it without help.

Independent reading sets the stage for *Linking Mode* later, as the student's abilities mature. With a strong (stable) foundation in the technical aspects of reading, the student becomes confident in *how* to read, which makes it possible to eventually add meaning and expressive qualities.

The better the reading and instrumental technique, the more opportunity for expression and interpretation.

The Hierarchy of Rhythm in Instrumental Music

It is generally accepted that students should fully understand the rhythm at one level before proceeding on to the next. Here are the three basic levels of rhythmic knowledge in *Notational Mode*:

Level 1—One beat and greater (quarter, half, dotted half, and whole notes).

Level 2—Divisions of one beat (duplets, triplets, and quadruplets) and the dotted quarter note (because it requires understanding eighth notes).

Level 3—More complex systems of counting where notes other than the quarter note serve as the unit of beat (six-eight time, simple time versus compound time, cut time, and others).

Two Types of Hierarchy in Level 1 Rhythms

Here is something that I consider an unusual twist on our understanding of hierarchy as it applies to Level 1 rhythms. On this level only, it's correct for hierarchy to occur either from large to small or the reverse—small to large.

An example of large to small can be found in the *Elementary Rubank* books (for instrumental music lessons) where the student learns whole notes first, then half notes. and then quarter notes.

The other type of hierarchy (from small to large) is found in most—but not all—piano lesson books for beginners, which teach quarter notes first, then half notes and whole notes.

Both of these styles are acceptable and correct for learning Level 1 rhythms because they both follow a form of hierarchy that leads to stable knowledge.

Reinforcing the Student's Perception of Hierarchy

I use a special technique to reinforce the idea of hierarchy in symbolism. I ask young students to make a chart on a blank paper by drawing a whole note at the top of the page, followed underneath by the next smallest note, then the next smallest, etc. In one glance, I can tell from their answers if any part of their understanding of hierarchy is missing or misunderstood.

By learning note values in hierarchical order, students more easily remember *the names* of the music symbols as well as their meaning. They can associate symbol names with fractional parts of the whole note: "Whole" (for whole note) means *the whole thing* or *all*. "Half" is *half* of the whole note. And "quarter" is a *quarter* of a whole note.

References to pizza pies, to the dollar, or to a large chocolate candy bar have been very effective in my classroom helping children visualize the fractional concepts of whole, half, and quarter.

Operational Hierarchy in Structured Music

Counting and processing rhythm for reading music is learned in a series of small incremental steps that train instrumental technique, eye techniques, and understanding of steady beat. This is what I consider *opera-*

tional knowledge and very different from *developmental knowledge* found in the creation of iconic notation (learning how symbols evolve).

Even the extraordinary accomplishments of Frank Lloyd Wright began with a single brick, a single board, a single line on a piece of paper. So, too, the concepts in reading music are built and formed by small, irrefutable steps the student can rely on for life.

My favorite way of teaching children to read and count rhythms in Notational Mode is beginning with quarter notes so the student learns to produce one short sound for each beat in a measure. This primitive level of reading music does not require counting—just see a note, play a note. If the student is playing on an adult-sized instrument for the first time, one sound per beat may be all the student is capable of at first. Whether the student taps quarter notes on a piano key, plucks them on a string, or plays them by using the tongue to interrupt the air flow on a woodwind or brass instrument, those physical movements provide the student with a strong kinesthetic experience of playing sound linked to the beat. I consider this the first step in the hierarchy of reading rhythm.

The second small step involves mentally counting numbers while producing those same sounds. Some students need a few weeks to learn this skill. It introduces the mathematical concept of *how many*. The student presses a key, blows a long tone, or moves the bow *while counting numbers*. The concept of counting beats is hierarchically higher than just playing tones on a steady beat.

Why are these first two steps important? They are the foundation of stable knowledge in rhythm. Everything else learned afterward is true because these elements are true. The beat is steady. The beat receives numbered counts. The student's first job is to master the ability to demonstrate both of these principles. While the student is mastering these two elements of training, the lesson book provides variety by introducing songs comprised of two or three pitches. In this manner, the student is never bored learning to count because the song pitches change each week, while keeping the counting requirements very simple.

This is the reading level that is appropriate for PreK and kindergarten classes. Small posters containing short pitched and non-pitched samples can be placed around the general music classroom next to various instruments for students to try out.

Boosting Students' Ability to Count While Playing

A teacher can tell right away in a private music lesson if the student is actually paying attention to numbered counts in a measure or just guessing at duration of tones by noticing how the student plays half notes and whole notes. The instant the teacher notices these symbols are not receiving their full value, the teacher can assume the student is not counting beats. Vague or faulty duration is usually an indicator that numbers are not being silently spoken in the student's mind while performing music.

Rather than alarm or discourage the student, I correct their counting by quietly pointing out that I notice they are not counting. Sometimes I ask them if they would put a cake in an oven and walk away without setting a timer? When they reply that they would not, I explain that this is similar to not timing a music note. And then I joke with them that the cake might be soggy (less time) or smoke might protrude from the oven (too much time).

Another indication that the student is not counting is if they play the incorrect number of repeated tones. If the measure calls for four quarter notes on the same pitch and the student plays three or five, the student is obviously not using a number system to keep track of the beats in the measure.

For this, I usually begin correcting them by complimenting things they are doing right. I mention their correct pitches and the fact that they played the entire song. Then I add, "I noticed you had too many (or too few) notes in this measure. Try it again, but this time say the counts for every measure in your mind as you play."

A Trick to Build a Student's Counting Ability

Self-motivation is so much better than a teacher nagging and begging a student to count duration. Instead, this method encourages self-reliance as the student establishes his or her own permanent *habit* of counting.

Here is a quick exercise in music dictation that almost instantly inspires a student to mentally keep track of counts. The student is seated at a table or desk with a blank sheet of paper and pencil. The teacher explains the directions: "The first time you hear the sample of music, just listen. The second time, write the example on paper. The third time, check your answer."

The student is then told that for each clap the teacher demonstrates, they should draw a vertical mark I call a 'stick mark'. The vertical stick marks will proceed left to right as if printing a series of lower case L's. The teacher then claps to a steady beat for five, seven, or nine beats. After allowing the student to hear the example two more times, the teacher asks the student how many stick marks they wrote down.

If the student isn't silently counting, the student's answer for the number of sticks will most likely be incorrect. The teacher can then ask the student to draw a box around their completed answer (to show that it is finished) and get ready to try again.

By repeating the stick exercise, the student will quickly learn to count numbers in their mind—on their own—in order to come up with the right answer.

Placing the sound upon the steady beat is the brick and mortar of reading written music. As students learn to properly count beats, they develop the understanding that *steady beat* lies beneath the notation, as a guide or template. This reinforces the idea that the beat is always present as the *foundation* for performing music.

After learning Level 1 rhythms, the student can then proceed to Level 2 rhythms where the beat is divided.

A Spatial Intelligence Method for Reading Rhythm

Throughout this book, we have been discussing the way we read pitches from the music staff using spatial intelligence. Reading rhythms is the same—it also requires spatial intelligence. No matter what type of symbols are being read, no matter what information is gathered from the symbols, spatial intelligence Part 1 helps the person recognize the shape, distance, and direction of the symbols. Spatial intelligence Part 2 helps the person transfer information from the written notation to the musical instrument.

The controversy surrounding how rhythms on the page should be taught lies in whether the person should be thinking about sounds in order to transfer the information or whether the person should be fully immersed in spatial aspects of the rhythm.

Aural methods for reading rhythm keep the person aware of vocal sounds through the use of rhythmic solfege, which assigns short syllables such as "Du" or "Ta" to a note value (quarter note, half note, etc.). Then, every time the person sees the quarter note in the music, they first remember the assigned vocal syllable and how the teacher demonstrated the duration of that syllable. This system of reading rhythms can work but only if the person becomes fluent in reading this way—which requires training and practice. I believe that aural learners would be more motivated to use this method than visual or kinesthetic learners because it heavily relies on aural perception and memory.

Spatial intelligence methods for reading music, which I recommend, do not rely on remembered sounds or syllables. Instead, they treat duration as distance—an obvious element of spatial reasoning. Rather than reading rhythms in a linear fashion as in aural methods, the person reading spatially is continuously aware of a down and up motion on every beat. These motions are referred to as the downbeat and the upbeat within each pulse of steady beat. The most traditional use of down-up counting is the practice of tapping the toe on every beat of music.

There are two advantages to perceiving these down-up spatial subdivision of the beat:

1. When the duration of sound is processed as distance—the length of the sound is perceived along the downward path or the upward path of the steady pulse. In other words, a quarter note lasts all the way through the downbeat and upbeat. An eighth note lasts through either a downbeat or upbeat, because an eighth note takes up only half a beat. Through this system, the person who is reading notation can always figure out their own rhythms once they know how much of the downbeat or upbeat to use. Therefore, it is very easy to sightread even complicated rhythms without help once the system is understood; this builds confidence in reading notation.

2. Down-up counting produces *anchored sounds* and *anacruses*, which contribute to musical energy in the performance. The downbeat is an anchored sound—it sounds firmly planted, solid, the way a person sits down in a chair. The upbeat is an anacrusis—it sounds as if it is lifting, lightly, the way a person gets up from a chair.

   Even more than that, the upbeat acts as the introduction to the next beat, the same way a person steps on a porch to step into a house. The house is the main element. You can have a house without a porch. But the reason the porch exists is to give you a platform by which to enter the house. If you play an upbeat correctly, it acts as a platform from which to launch into the next beat.

The anacrusis effect can be felt in the word "Hel-lo." Notice that "-lo" is the strongest part of the word with the heaviest emphasis. It acts as an anchor beat because it is strongly felt. "Hel-" would be the upbeat (acting as a porch) to step into the "-lo" down beat (which acts as the house).

"-Lo" might be written as a quarter note with "Hel-" as an eighth note preceding it.

The energy in the down-up system of reading rhythms is created because the musician is switching back and forth between opposing forces to create the energy. Down and up are opposites, as are yin and yang, push and pull, expand and contract.

I'm not sure the same energy can be obtained by using aural methods with rhythmic solfege syllables. The visualization of the beat is not the same. Also, it takes far more effort to learn rhythmic syllables and keep referring to them in music lessons than to use the down-up concepts, which are as close at hand as the student's foot and their tapping toe. Perhaps that is why most instrumental teachers use the down-up system of visualizing the beat.

As a practical matter, it's common to sightread a piece of music by singing syllables for pitch (Do, Re, Mi, etc.) while using the down-up counting method. However, it would be *impossible* to vocalize (or even think about) syllables for pitch solfege (Do, Re, Mi) while also using syllables for rhythmic solfege (Ta, Ta, Ti, Ti, Ta) at the same time.

This entire discussion demonstrates the difficulty of introducing a notational reading program in PreK and Kindergarten if the general music teacher teaching it has only been trained in aural rhythmic syllables. At first, that teacher may not be in favor of switching to the spatial down-up counting system for early grades because of such a strong belief in the aural system. And yet, that is exactly what children will need in order to fully grasp the progression of hierarchically based rhythmic knowledge.

If teachers are shown the research about training the longer neural pathways and what I have written here about the advantages of down-up counting, they would hopefully be willing to learn and implement spatial reading skills in early grades. Otherwise, schools may be left with no other option than to set up additional music classes that are only taught by instrumental teachers, who routinely teach notation using spatial concepts that are effective.

As difficult as that may seem at first to establish new or additional music classes in school, we must remember that huge national initiatives like breakfast programs and ESOL programs for immigrant children were once initially pilot programs before later becoming federally funded. They grew from a desire for better learning conditions for certain groups of students. Reading music is no different except for the fact that it would be intended to improve the cognition of *every child* rather than just a select group.

The Loop Counting System

Something I call 'The Loop Counting System' is a further adaptation of the foot-tapping method. I also refer to it as 'The Wickstrom Method', named for Professor Carl Wickstrom from Ithaca College School of Music who taught it extensively to all of us instrumental methods students in the 1960s. At Ithaca, we were required to demonstrate proficiency in clapping the down-up directions of rhythms as well as draw directional symbols beneath written notation. These techniques are very useful when combined with rhythm dictation. I owe much of my success as a teacher to this method because my students usually become very confident sight-readers.

One thing I forgot to mention is that throughout the down-up visualization, the student is taught to use the number system of counting, such as counting "One, two, three, four" in every measure in 4/4 time. Then when beats are divided, duplets are referred to as "One-and," triplets are called "One-and-and," and quadruplets are called "One-ee-and-uh."

Sometimes this basic number system seems too abstract for young children and doesn't resonate with them, so I learned to use word examples for young children (and even adults, when necessary). In this method, syllables are employed instead of numbers: the duplet sounds like "apple," triplets sound line "blue-ber-ry," and quadruplets sound like "peanut-but-ter." For quarter notes, we say "pie." This keeps the idea of "fun" in the lesson while learning to associate the sound of these divisions of the beat with language the student is already familiar with.

But eventually, I make sure all students know the correct names for notation by pointing to notation with a pencil saying words like "Quarter, eight-eight, quarter, rest."

Notice that in each instance, I state a reason for each method. I do not use syllables that have no meaning in and of themselves like "Du" or "Ta" as in the aural method because they would require more time and, in my view, don't qualify as stable knowledge.

We can't send students out into the world forever referring to notation as "Ta-ta-ti-ti-ta." Eventually, rhythmic syllables still have to be replaced with a number counting system in order to keep track of where the rhythm occurs within a measure. So why not just use a numbered system in the first place?

(For an in-depth description of 'The Loop Counting System', see **Addendum 4:** *The Loop System of Counting*.)

Hierarchy in Pitch Knowledge

In *Notational Mode*, hierarchy applies not just to the order required in learning to read pitches but to general pitch knowledge as well. For instance, the pitches in scales and keys are more easily understood and remembered if they are taught in the order found in the Circle of Fifths. By starting out with no sharps and no flats (Key of C) and then adding only one sharp or one flat, the student sees scales and keys as a *progressive plan*.

The one drawback to starting out in the key of C is that we always have to explain the ledger line (C_4) below the staff. That may be the reason why I've seen early reading lessons in general music start out using the keys of F and G and avoiding C—because the keys of F and G place Do, Re, and Mi in the middle area of the music staff thereby avoiding notes below the staff on ledger lines.

An even better strategy for teaching children to read in the middle of the treble staff might be to start out in the key of "a-minor," which (just like C

Major) requires no sharps or flats. By starting in a-minor, students could become very proficient in reading from the staff before dealing with the addition of sharps and flats in the keys of G or F. Hierarchically, we would be teaching simple reading skills (no sharps or flats) before skills that are more complex.

The key of a-minor also places Do, Re, and Mi on the letters A, B, C—an *order of letters* which children find much more logical to remember than C-D-E (the first three tones in the key of C) or F-G-A (Key of F) or G-A-B (Key of G).

Hierarchy in Review

In summary, it's important to follow strict hierarchy in Notational Mode for Level I, II, and III rhythms, for teaching individual symbols before patterns of symbols, and for teaching the pitches of scales and keys in order.

We must remember that in aural mode, hierarchy is not essential because aural neural pathways are already present and just need experience and discovery in order to thicken. In aural mode, a person can imitate and improvise in any key at any time. In contrast, visual processing requires simple forms of knowledge first, leading into more complex forms, in order to build the solid foundation for multiple long neural pathways that will travel to the highest levels of cognition.

Chapter 8

Abstraction and Symbolism

Most music educators agree there is one true impediment standing in the way of programs for young children to learn to read music notation—their lack of abstract reasoning. When children enter school at four or five years of age, the part of their brain that processes abstractions has not yet been fully formed.

We have known this since at least the 1950s due to the work of Swiss Developmental Psychologist **Jean Piaget** (1896-1980), who is remembered as the first psychologist to make a systematic study of cognitive development. Piaget recognized that children did not have the full ability to use symbols relating to abstract concepts until age twelve, basing his beliefs on observing children's behavior. Today through medical imaging, scientists are able to track these changes in the brain as children mature from birth through age twenty-five.

Piano Lessons for PreK Students

Written music contains so many abstractions that, for years, piano teachers were more apt to start children on piano during the latter half of their kindergarten year or in first grade, rather than earlier. By then, students seemed mature enough to begin reading from the staff.

However, not all parents and teachers were willing to wait for children to mature. Some wanted to give musically gifted children a head start in reading music, during the pre-school years, before children became immersed in the pressures and requirements of attending school.

Some music educators have devised number systems, color systems, or rote learning systems for children to read music early. These methods can be moderately successful because children can learn songs for the piano—but they don't lead to understanding standard notation or develop the ability to read independently from the music staff.

What's the Hurry?

Why are some parents and educators so interested in teaching note-reading to children earlier and earlier while others are convinced children should spend their early years developing aural skills first? Is it even advisable for children to learn visual music skills so early on? What would be the benefits of reading music early? Let's recall what we know of behaviors in young children and compare that to our new knowledge of how neural pathways form in the brain.

As previously mentioned, the skills in Aural Mode such as imitating, responding to pitches, vocalizing pitches, and listening to music are present almost from birth. These short neurons will thicken and become more effective through use, exploration, and discovery. The child will continue to develop aural processing through everyday activities and through targeted activities in general music class. The fact that aural skills are an inherent part of childhood development is precisely why they are called *natural* abilities in music. Therefore, it is reasonable to assume that these natural abilities may require training, but they are not in danger of requiring urgent intervention in order to develop.

Notational reading skills are just the opposite. They are not apparent at birth or an automatic part of childhood. This is because the long neural pathways that carry the necessary spatial intelligence information required for visual recognition of shape, distance, and direction must be stimulated and established through exact repetition. Unlike aural skills, notational skills require intervention and instruction through planned year-by-year programs for the development of neural pathways used in staff reading.

A significant portion of brain development occurs before kindergarten. So PreK is the perfect year in school to begin the development of new brain cells leading to higher order thinking and visual processing—while the child's brain is still involved in significant growth.

But the question still remains—how do we overcome a child's deficiencies in abstract processing at that age in order to introduce the abstract concepts in music notation?

New Solutions Overcoming Abstractions

Young children have been known to understand one abstract thought at a time but are less likely to understand or use two or three abstractions at once.

When I first became aware of this in college, I wondered what this had to do with music. What elements of music are abstract? In order to understand this, we have to see the world through a child's eyes. Children live in the concrete, tangible world. They understand things that can be experienced by touching, eating, throwing, etc.—words such as ball, toy, pillow, dish, etc.

But if you give them an abstract word about something intangible that they can't hold in their hand, they have nothing to compare it to. Children can't eat or throw a whole note. To them, a "rest" means to take a nap. A "note" is something you give the bus driver. Many of the terms we use in music belong in the adult world but have no point of reference in a child's world.

Another abstract concept that children have a difficult time with is the five-line staff. The lines are not a problem for children because they look similar to the rungs of a ladder. But the spaces between the lines, on the other hand, are a different matter. After all, every child knows that on a ladder, there is "nothing" in between the rungs. Yet we try to tell children that the blank area between staff lines is "something," not "nothing." It makes no sense to children why adults treat the white, blank areas between staff lines as if they are usable. The idea that an empty area is something real is an abstract concept. That's why young children who are asked to write the letter names on the music staff will only write letters on the lines, at first, and ignore the spaces completely.

One way to help them to place value on the spaces is to use a marker or crayon to color each space between the lines so students can see them . . . and then give the colored spaces (or "stripes") their alphabet name.

The key to teaching young children to read music is to identify all the abstractions they will encounter and modify them. In order for our schools to institute notational reading in early grades, general music teachers will need to learn how to modify abstractions by associating them with concrete ideas.

The Companion Words Method

One question that has puzzled me is: Can I teach *young* children the *real* process of reading music—rather than using a fake music game or temporary gimmick that promises much but delivers little in terms of lasting knowledge or ability?

What I discovered through extensive work with children ages five and younger, is that they are just as capable of reading music as older students if some temporary accommodations are made for them early in the process.

As I closely examined the abilities of younger children over time, a method emerged that fits all of my criteria—one that teaches real symbols and real concepts. I call it **The Companion Words Method**.

By *temporarily* substituting concrete names for abstract labels, I've been able to guide children to read from the staff in a way that's meaningful and comfortable for them. The old way of teaching them—using adult terms, having them memorize vocabulary words they don't understand, as well as lines and spaces of the staff—has never worked well for the very young. Instead, Companion Words uses the logic of an interesting story, allowing the child's imagination to become a vehicle to higher order thinking. What's more, it pushes all the right emotional and psychological buttons of love and empathy with the story characters that help students associate warm, meaningful experiences with the structured learning process.

Three Components of a Musical Symbol

Let's take a look at the three components of a music symbol—the **shape**, the **action**, and the **name**. (These three components are not a new idea. For instance, educational theorist **Jerome Bruner** [1915-2016] envisioned knowledge as being *enactive, iconic,* and *symbolic*, which are basically synonymous to my terms. However, I think my model is easier to understand and implement.)

Here is how my terms can be used to understand the components of a whole note:

- Its **shape** is a circle.
- Its **action** requires making a sound on the instrument for four counts (in 4/4 time).
- Its **name** is "whole note."

I found that four- and five-year-old children could easily differentiate the circle *shape* from other shapes like triangles, rectangles, and squares. Therefore, *shape recognition* was not a problem.

I also found that children could remember and perform the *action* of pressing a piano key when I pointed to a circle. They also avoided pressing the piano key for other shapes. They had no trouble counting the duration of the whole note using numbers. Therefore, *executing the action* was not a problem.

However, when I referred to the symbol by its formal name, children had difficulty recalling the names *whole note, half note,* and *quarter note.* They had trouble associating note names with symbol shapes. And, in reverse, they could not consistently tell me the number of counts a symbol received when I referred to the symbol by its formal name. If I continued the lesson by using the formal names of music symbols, the child became uninterested in the lesson, somewhat agitated, and unenthused. From these observations, we can conclude that children can easily form a strong association between shape and action, but they have difficulty attaching meaning when it comes to naming the symbol.

Finally, I understood the specific aspect of a music symbol that was keeping young children from reading music—*the name given to each symbol in standard notation.*

Naming is an advanced, abstract, and adult concept. The names for symbols that we adults have contrived have no relevance in the world of a small child. When we say "whole," the child may think "hole," like the hole a rabbit goes into. Likewise, the child has no reference for "note," as it applies to music. To a child, a note is a piece of paper with something written on it.

The next step for me was to provide age-appropriate language that made sense to children in order to teach music concepts. I theorized that the three properties of the music symbol—**shape**, **action**, and **name**— would become unified if I temporarily replaced the adult-abstract concept of "whole note on the C ledger line" with a concrete word, such as "cat," because we can call the ledger line (for C_4, written below the treble staff) the cat's "whiskers."

Children already knew how to find the "cat" key (C_4, Middle C) on the piano. We talked about Middle C as "the place where the cat lives." From here, associating "CATs" from the written page to the correct key on the piano seemed natural and even fun for four- and five-year-old students.

Children quickly learned to press the "CAT" key for four beats if I pointed to a whole note on the C_4 ledger line. The next step was to take a look at the "DOG" (a whole note on D_4), which does not have a "whisker" line going through the middle of it. I then showed the child four-note examples of whole notes randomly made up of "CATs" and "DOGs"—examples using C_4 and D_4. Most children played these patterns correctly the first time.

The child was not playing C's and D's by color; I was not using a rote method where we clapped the pattern first and imitated the pitches and rhythms. Instead, I presented them with a visual note pattern they had never seen before made up of C's and D's, and they independently read and interpreted the pattern for the piano. That's what real reading is. And it's the type of reading that music literacy is based on.

In the second lesson we learned that when the white CAT (circle shape, whole note) was holding a pole, it meant to press the piano key for two counts (a half note). If the CAT was black and carrying a pole, it meant to press the key for one count (quarter note).

The more I used Companion Words, the easier it became to invent imaginary reasons for the shapes the students and I saw on the page. My make-believe characters easily wove themselves into a whimsical story that the children and I both enjoyed.

The best part was how easily children read from the staff when imagination was involved. The second best part was how the characters and story never became a permanent crutch because it wasn't long before the children were calling the "CATs" and "DOGs" by their real names, "C" and "D." And third, my favorite aspect was the way I could maintain the child's dignity and restore confidence if they forgot any of the letter names just by mentioning the concrete character names again.

The Companion Words Method is based on five premises:

1. By replacing the abstract name for a music symbol with a concrete name (a companion word), children four and five years old can use symbolism right away to read notation from the music staff.

2. An age-appropriate story with companion words acts as a temporary bridge that helps a child build new symbolic and abstract neural pathways.

3. Through concrete names and imagination, a child can develop abstract reasoning two or three years earlier than the expected age of seven—thereby beginning the process of reading music during the optimal years for learning, instead of waiting.

4. Companion words for learning music notation help students develop the spatial abilities needed for academic learning much earlier.

5. The Companion Words Method is ideal for private instrumental lessons, but it can also be easily adapted for a general music classroom by having the children perform the written music on student xylophones or singing the tones from the music staff.

Abstract Concepts through Companion Words

For several years, I experimented and developed the Companion Words method with young piano students and even adapted a modified version for adults. I learned to be *inventive*. I found that any abstract idea that previously acted as a roadblock could be explained through imagination.

For instance, I used creative story elements to explain how the Middle C ledger line appears to "float" on the page from the treble area to the bass area of the staff, while representing the same piano key (C_4). Not only is the floating line between the staves an odd concept to explain or understand—even for older students—but it's taught in beginning lessons when children have the *least amount of capacity* to understand even basic concepts.

Regardless, this became very easy to explain through The Companion Words Method. Sometimes "the cat that lived under the building (on the treble clef) went on vacation down to Bass Clef Land to visit the bear (the B whole note on top of the bass clef)." When I used this imaginary visual, children immediately understood that even when Middle C "travels," it is always Middle C, no matter whether it's written close to the upper staff or lower staff.

The 2015 Amherst Study for Hierarchy

Little did I know that at the same time I was experimenting with Companion Words, the 2015 Amherst study I referenced in the beginning pages of this book was measuring neural pathways that included *imagination* and *abstractions*.

As previously mentioned, the aim of the 2015 study published by P. Taylor, J. N. Hobbs, J. Burroni, and H.T. Siegelmann was to prove or disprove the hierarchical order of cognitive abilities in the brain. They also wanted to know if abstract neural pathways went further into the brain than concrete ones.

This study used resting state functional magnetic resonance imaging (rs-fMRI) and diffusion tensor imaging (DTI) to observe and record the length of neural pathways and connectivity between regions of the brain as they responded to skills and activities.

The study reported that some types of information consistently traveled to regions closest to the data entry point where the information enters the brain on shorter neural pathways. Other information consistently went deeper into the brain on longer neural pathways.

The study produced a chart showing a pyramid of five gradients of cognition. The beginning level, at the bottom, showed sensory cortical inputs near the data entry points. From there, the pyramid rises upward through four more levels.

The fifth level, at the peak, contained *deep symbolic content.* It was farthest from the data entry point and required the longest neural pathways. The study called this area the "pinnacle of the human brain network." It dealt with *imagination*, language, *concepts*, *naming*, reasoning, and humor (all attributes that are present in The Companion Words Method).

On the bottom level of the pyramid, closest to the data entry points, were tangible language-related elements and aural processing, including speech execution, *musical cognition*, *whistling*, *auditory discrimination*, *music comprehension and production*, *pitch*, *prosody*, and *auditory perception.*

(To compare the findings of this study with the national [voluntary] music goals, see **Addendum 2:** *The National Music Goals in Relation to Reading Music.*)

Implications for Early Childhood Education

Here are some conclusions we can draw from the 2015 Amherst study:

1. Imagination, naming, and abstract concepts, as well as humor, reside in the deepest area of the brain, at the top of the hierarchy of cognitive processing.

2. This study provides scientific evidence that imagination information travels on neural pathways that go to the same section of the brain as *naming* and *deep symbolic content*. This supports the idea that four- and five-year-olds can, indeed, learn to read music symbols through imagination.

3. The close proximity of naming and imagination (at the farthest point from data entry), makes it logical to theorize that heavily traveled neural pathways for imagination could stimulate growth of new pathways for naming and abstract thought. That would explain why we see children—who start out using child-appropriate Companion Words—later naturally switch over to using the adult-type formal names for music symbols *on their own*. (This is *provided* the teacher has correctly followed the principles of The

Companion Words Method by always introducing new concepts with both the child's word and the adult's word. Examples: "This is a staff, but we are going to call it a building," or "This is a whole note, but we are going to call it a cat.")

4. When we train children in *Aural Mode*, we help them develop the sensory skills that are closest to incoming data in the brain. When we train children in *Notational Mode*, we help them to read standard notation with skills that are deep in the brain, at the highest levels of cognition.

The implication for school districts is that music programs that exclusively train aural skills and music intelligence are only training students' shortest neural pathways and not developing their longer neural pathways for *naming* and *deep symbolic content*—the same type of skills required for reading and writing English.

This study, along with my teaching experience, has solidified my belief that there is no impediment that would keep four- and five-year-old children from learning to read symbols on the music staff if we were to use age-appropriate methods in the music classroom. Young students may not have the physical strength to hold a full-sized instrument and join a band or orchestra, but they can certainly sing and vocalize the rhythm they are reading. And they can use smaller-sized pitched instruments such as student xylophones for reading notation in the classroom. In doing so, they are not only developing music literacy but higher order thinking skills, as well. See **Addendum 5:** *Classroom Management for Student Xylophones.*

Teaching Abstractions in Early Childhood

By stimulating imagination through Companion Words, we no longer need to wait for children's full cognitive development (age 7 to 12), to begin teaching children how to read standard notation. As soon as the child has working memory (developed around age four), the child can recognize music symbols and transfer the information to a simple pitched instrument.

Teaching Music Symbols in Early Childhood

1. **Associate the symbol shape with action**—once the child can differentiate one shape from another, the instructor helps the child associate a symbol's shape with the expected action. (Example: Introduce the "circle" shape of the whole note and ask the student to press a piano key for four counts.)

2. **Engage the child's imagination when introducing symbolism**—the instructor helps the student experience properties of the symbol shape through Companion Words and an age-appropriate story. (Example: The student can always identify C_4 [Middle C] in the printed music by looking for the cat's whisker line [the C_4 ledger line].)

3. **Allow the natural transition from concrete to abstract terms**—the instructor frequently uses the adult's abstract term along with the child's concrete term until the Companion Word fades from use. Children naturally want to use adult words and will do so once they understand what they mean. *Meaning* in imagination leads to *meaning* in abstraction. (Example: the child starts out calling C_4 the "cat" but soon *prefers* to call it "C" and then "Middle-C.")

The Companion Words Script

The easiest way—perhaps a foolproof way—to teach Companion Words is through the Companion Words Script. The teacher can be relaxed and confident when the correct delivery of the material is all printed out. By reading the script to the class, teachers can teach children about the music staff whether the teacher is trained in music or not. For instance, a nursery-school teacher could use Companion Words to increase students' spatial intelligence abilities for all types of reading. The Companion Words Script can be used verbatim or serve as an example for the teacher to make up a similar story.

As the teacher uses the script to engage children's imagination, the teacher should be aware of two important spatial intelligence concepts children also learn from the story—location and duration.

Regarding *location*, it's difficult for young children to know what is meant by notes that are "under the staff" or "on the first line." The Companion Words story reinforces these location concepts by saying that the "cat" and "dog" (C_4 and D_4) live *under the building* (under the staff). And by saying that "eagle" flies down to perch on the *first step* of the building (E_4).

You can test this yourself. Ask young students who have been reading and playing Middle-C notes to draw a whole note on the Middle-C line under the treble staff. Invariably, the students will ignore the word "under" and draw the Middle-C whole note somewhere up on the staff lines and spaces. Why? Because to a child, lines mean "where you write or print." Unless the concept of "below the staff" has been taught and tested, we can't assume that young learners have acquired stable knowledge of Middle C's location.

Another important concept presented in the Companion Words story is *duration*. At first the students learn that the cat is a round circle with a "whisker line" (a Middle C whole note on a ledger line). But as I mentioned earlier, it takes only minutes to show them the same Middle C can be a "white cat with a pole" (half note) and "black cat with a pole" (quarter note). These new forms of "cat" are still identifiable because they all use the whisker line going through the circle part. The only thing that makes them different is their colors or shapes that indicate how long to press the piano key (duration).

(The complete script for Companion Words is provided at the back of this book in **Addendum 6:** *Introducing Companion Words in Early Childhood.*)

Time Requirements for Companion Words

One way to incorporate the Companion Words Method in the PreK classroom a little at a time is to include this simple music story in ten- or fifteen-minute segments as part of the morning circle. In addition, the spatial recognition of music symbols can also be incorporated into reading readiness activities for English, such as cutting and pasting shapes.

Why only learn letters and numbers when you can also learn a few music symbols such as quarter notes and rests, or whole and half notes?

In general music class, a few minutes training a student's spatial skills for reading music symbols through games or activity centers reinforces children's spatial skills not only for music but for reading English. In the same regard, spatial activities in English literacy reinforce spatial skills for reading music notation; they complement each other.

By simultaneously teaching music literacy and English literacy in the early grades, we are also enhancing higher order cognitive abilities for processing symbols and abstractions. When you combine spatial abilities and higher order abilities, you have two major reasons to teach music literacy and English literacy side by side in the early grades.

Chapter 9

The Importance of Process

As just discussed, children can be introduced to reading music over time, through small sequential steps that are incorporated into the general music curriculum from PreK on. Or, they can be introduced to music notation quickly when they sign up for private lessons or join a beginning instrumental program. I call the quick method the All-At-Once introduction to reading notation.

Learning to read music does not require prior singing ability or months of rhythm training. As long as the student can hear and clap back a simple rhythm pattern, knows the alphabet, and is willing to learn, the student has all the tools they need to begin building the long neurons that are the foundation of notational reading.

There are major differences between the Over-Time Method and the All-At-Once Method. In the Over-Time Method found in general music programs, there is no home practice requirement. The student learns to read notation on instruments that are easy to manage such as student xylophones or recorders.

The All-At-Once Method is quite the opposite; it is designed for adult-type instruments. It follows a prescribed plan of successive lessons presented in a beginning lesson book, and it requires about three hours of home practice per week (thirty minutes daily, for six days).

Kinesthetic Training that Precedes the All-At-Once Method

While aural abilities are not involved in the initial stages of building the long neurons necessary for reading music notation, aural abilities are extremely helpful when wind or string instrumental students are first introduced to their adult-type instrument. Before learning to read notation, these students need instruction understanding how the instrument is assembled, how to hold it during performance, how to make the proper sound, and how to form their fingers (or slide positions) for the first pitches shown in their first lesson book. This instruction could take up to two, three, or four lessons depending on the opinion of the instructor as to when the students are ready to move on to reading notation. To offset the drudgery of concentrating on long tones, lip slurs, or bowing techniques that develop characteristic tone quality, students can use their aural music abilities on the short neurons to play very simple familiar songs right away, such as "Hot Cross Buns," "Mary Had a Little Lamb," or "Twinkle, Twinkle Little Star."

In addition to learning songs by imitation and rote, students can also be asked to teach themselves to play one of the songs by sounding out the tones they have learned. Usually the instructor helps the students "find" the first three or more tones, which the students write down using alphabet letters. Then, for home practice, the students are encouraged to guess and try out pitches until they discover the rest of the song, which they will write down and bring back to the next class.

These early exercises with familiar songs accomplish two things. First, they provide the student with the more immediate personal satisfaction of being able to play songs for family and friends that are easily recognizable. Second, they provide the time and experience necessary for the student to control the instrument and the sound before engaging in the visual and cognitive skills of reading notation.

Once sound production and fingerings are almost second nature, the student will easily be able to begin reading notation in a beginning lesson book.

But, beware! Not all students will be good at "sounding out" a new song; and if the student seems especially anxious or frustrated, these early aural-type exercises can be skipped entirely. There is nothing wrong with starting in the lesson book at the first lesson.

Why Piano Students Begin Differently

Unlike beginning wind and string students who are physically challenged at first with the size and mechanics of the instrument, piano students require only a few minutes of instruction about the piano keys in order to begin reading from their lesson book.

Processing Notation for the First Time

When a student has no prior experience reading music, the goal during the first lesson in the All-At-Once Method should be to treat reading notation not so much as a *sequential* process as a *simultaneous* one—similar to learning how to ride a two-wheel bike. Whether learning to ride a bike or learning to read music, success ultimately depends on the student learning to monitor all skill areas at once in order to keep moving forward.

The moment the bike wheels begin to move, the cyclist is managing four things at once: steering, looking ahead, operating the pedals, and balancing to stay vertical. Cyclists may be filled with frustration and anxiety at first, especially if they attempt to focus on just their feet or just their hands. When this happens, the bike and rider fall over. Focusing on just one area doesn't work on a bike because that requires taking the mind off of all other areas—which usually results in disaster.

In a similar manner, the student reading music has to balance playing to a steady beat, simultaneously reading pitch and duration from the staff, and finding finger locations (or slide positions) on the instrument.

This is why learning to read music *while* playing an instrument can be overwhelming on the first day—because different cognitive processes must operate simultaneously in order to achieve success. This sounds terribly complicated but, in reality, it's not. Amazingly, the brain is capable of gearing up quickly if the student is briefly introduced beforehand to the three vital components of reading notation:

- Duration of notes according to ***steady beat***
- Some alphabetic/pitch knowledge on ***the music staff***
- Some alphabetic/pitch knowledge on ***the instrument***

After retiring from teaching in public schools, I still found ways to teach music—for afterschool piano programs, summer programs, music shops, and music agencies. All the students who came to me for instruction, no matter what age or grade level, had little or no prior experience reading music, which I found incredible considering that these children had attended public school general music instruction for years. To accommodate the time constraints set by the music agencies, my introductory lessons became brief and streamlined. Sometimes the family only paid for a twenty-minute lesson for their child. Eventually, I learned to cover all the major points required to get a new student into their new lesson book in record time.

Here's the "magic formula" I used:

Introducing Steady Beat. First, I'd spend a few minutes teaching simple rhythm dictation using quarter notes and quarter rests, so the student would understand the relationship between the sounds of the notes and the steady pulse of the music. Each time I clapped my hands, they would draw a vertical stick (representing the stem of a quarter note) on their paper. For each non-clapped beat (hands thrown apart), they would draw a vertical squiggle mark (representing a quarter rest). I would then demonstrate several examples of four-beat patterns of notes and rests. Next, I showed them how sounds can last for two beats or four beats by clasping my hands together while counting "1, 2" or "1, 2, 3, 4." Through these visual examples, the student gained confidence, as this information was easier to understand.

Reviewing the Instrument. Second, we would review tones on the instrument. For brass, woodwinds, or strings, this would mean reviewing the two or three tones they had been using to play simple songs on their instrument. For piano students, we looked at the piano keyboard. We noticed how the black keys occurred in patterns of twos and threes. We located Middle C, D, and E with the right hand. We examined the alphabet recurring over and over, left to right, on the keys.

Introducing the Music Staff. Third, the student would learn to identify one, two, or three pitch locations on the staff (depending on their age and ability). These pitches, of course, would be the same pitches they were about to use for the first exercise in the lesson book.

The All-At-Once Method start-up process takes approximately twenty minutes. Yes, that's right—twenty minutes! Not weeks. Not months. And I have accomplished it in even less time, when needed.

Next, we'd open the lesson book, discuss what we saw on the page, and I'd stand back as the student played the first simple song or exercise *with minimal help from me.*

By the end of that first All-At-Once reading lesson, the student could set aside any initial fear and uncertainty. Instead of wondering if they would be successful, they now had the answers to their unspoken questions: *Will I be able to do it? Will I be able to read the notes? Will I be able to play the instrument correctly?*

There was a time, early in my teaching career, when I evaluated students by using aptitude tests because that was part of my college training. But experience soon taught me the chief factor for learning to read music is not aptitude—it's attitude.

In order to succeed at reading music, a person has to be willing to try, willing to fail, and willing to endure.

I have seen the slowest learner in the class outlast and outperform everyone else; I have also seen some very talented students quit easily. In instrumental music, we teach and manage character development in our students as much as we teach spatial and kinesthetic skills. We try to show students what they are capable of, what they can achieve, from the very first lesson.

When students leave their first music lesson, they should feel like they are already on the successful path—not because we *told* them they did a good job but because they witnessed their own ability to achieve success.

Remediating Deficiencies in Reading Music

Many people think of reading music as one ability. They refer to it as "taking lessons" or "playing an instrument." However, reading music involves many different types of cognition and skill sets within each area. When a student makes a mistake by playing a wrong note, the teacher should be equipped to evaluate why the mistake occurred. Quick remediation depends on the teacher's knowledge of exactly how music is read and how it is produced on the instrument.

One of the most important aspects of remediation is recognizing where an error occurred in the reading process. If an error occurred "locally," this means it occurred either on the staff or on the instrument. Did the error occur as the student looked at the music? Sometimes the student thinks the note was on the second line but it actually was on the third line—a sight error. Or did it occur when the student's hands or mouth were operating the instrument? For example, the fourth finger might not have reacted quickly enough or the student couldn't remember the fingering. By alerting the student as to where the error occurred, the student can think about exactly what they are doing wrong and how to correct it. Think how much better this type of remediation is than the vague and meaningless ways of correcting students like saying, "You just need to practice more until you can play the piece without mistakes."

The teacher also needs to know intuitively whether each mistake is a one-time accident or a recurring mistake that needs true remediation. Most of the time, I let one-time accidents go by without commenting, concentrating on the mistakes I am sure the student makes every time they play the piece. This helps me maximize the minutes in the lesson so I can help the student move forward in important tasks rather than dwell on something accidental.

Also, I don't have to comment on each individual accidental mistake because my overall plan in music lessons is to continually guide the student to use their eyes in such a way as to avoid unnecessary errors. For instance, we work on looking ahead in the music and examine the need to slow down the tempo to "give the eyes and the brain plenty of time to process the notes." In addition, when a student makes constant accidental mistakes even though a piece has been mastered, I often use the techniques outlined in *Chapter 13: Chronic Mistakes Syndrome*.

While some mistakes occur locally, others occur in the student's mind when the student transforms the staff information into instrument information. This is similar to the way MIDI translators change keyboard language into computer language. In reading music, the performer must transform the language of the music staff into the language of the instrument.

Spatial *transformation*, a feature of spatial intelligence, helps the student take information from one local area to another. A note written on the second space of the treble staff has to be transformed to fingering or position information in order to produce the tone. When I speak to students about this ability to transfer staff knowledge to the instrument, I call these *matching skills*. We match the "A" location for a note on the staff to the "A" fingering on the instrument.

Most students have played card games where they spread out all the cards face down and turn them over one by one, trying to find identical cards that "match." I've used this visual image to allay students' frustrations with reading mistakes by asking them to treat the process of reading notes as a matching game. Subsequently, they viewed the reading process as a challenging game, rather than putting unfair pressure on themselves to remember note names and play correct tones. The idea of playing a game helps them relax and enjoy their efforts to improve their reading skills.

Understanding Order in the Reading Process

We can easily learn to identify local skills and transformation skills by looking at how pitch and duration are processed. Being able to recognize pitch and duration at the same instant and perform pitch and duration as if they were one idea, instead of two different concepts, is the key to reading notation. This amazing ability of the brain begins in the very first lesson. Let me explain how this happens:

1. **Visual Recognition**—First, the student focuses on local skills **on the music staff** by recognizing a shape on the staff according to its alphabet name or by its location, such as "second line" (pitch information). At the same time, the student recognizes special visual characteristics of the note that pertain to duration. Is the note head black? White? Does it have a straight stem? No stem? A stem with a flag? Both of these ideas—pitch and duration—must be simultaneously understood for every note that is read so the brain is processing these two elements over and over throughout a piece of music. It is common for most students to grasp this ability right away during their very *first* music lesson. Remember how I said reading music was like riding a bike by managing many skills at once? The way a teacher knows if this simultaneous process is working correctly is by observing if the student can play in time to the steady beat, without stopping. The moment the student falters and stops, something has gone wrong with either reading the pitch or the duration. If the teacher can identify which part the student is unsure of, and offer some quick drill, the student will be able to continue reading properly.

2. **Transformation**—After recognizing pitch and duration simultaneously, the student silently (without using language) transforms

staff-type information into instrument-type information. For example, on the saxophone, the performer *transforms* the visual image of a staff shape (note on the second line written as a non-filled-in circle with a stem) into silent instantaneous directions such as "Cover the thumb hole plus two additional holes and make the sound last for two beats."

3. **Playing the Instrument**—Third, the student physically carries out the silent message mechanically on the instrument by making the instrument produce the correct tone for two beats.

These three steps in note reading happen so quickly—in a split second—that it may feel as if reading and playing are joined as one process. But as you see from the steps I described, they are not. Note recognition, transformation, and execution of the tone each require different cognitive processes in the brain. Knowing this helps the educator determine what is working or not working in the reading process and then address that particular concern.

It's also helpful to involve the student by saying, "Let's figure out what the problem might be. Were you unsure of what you saw on the staff?" If not, "Were you unsure of how to direct your hands?" And then perhaps, "Or were your hands unable to carry out the directions?"

The more you lead the student through this inquiry, the easier it will become for the student to pinpoint the cause of errors without the teacher's help.

Local Skills at the Staff Level

We don't hear mistakes as they occur at the local staff level, nor do we hear a mistake made mentally as the student transforms staff information into instrument information. Mistakes are *always* heard at the local area of the instrument where the sound is incorrectly played—in Step 3. That's when we first notice that something is wrong. And yet, the mistake may actually have occurred seconds before the sound was created—during Step 1 or

2. The effective music teacher will be able to point out the source of the error and offer remedial assistance to eliminate future errors of this kind.

Often, students complain that they have difficulty remembering the letter names of notes (a Step 1 error). Here is where the Companion Words Method can help young students associate visual images with alphabet letter names to make the letter names more concrete than abstract. In older students, memorization of the names of lines and spaces can be improved through mnemonics such as All-Cows-Eat-Grass (for memorizing the spaces of the bass clef).

Beyond issues with letter names, many more local staff mistakes are really the result of poorly developed eye-motion techniques, which incidentally is a strong point in favor of early eye exams in schools. For detailed information about eye-motion techniques, see *Chapter 10: Training the Eyes.*

Local Skills at the Instrument Level

Sometimes a student's reading ability at the staff level is excellent but the student fails to operate the instrument properly—a Step 3 problem. Posture, breathing, curvature of fingers, facial muscles used in embouchures, the angle and weight applied to a bow, learning the positions of a slide, etc. are all technical considerations that affect performance.

Other times, a student may be unsure of the fingering or position on the instrument. In order to keep the music going, they substitute a guess; often they guess incorrectly. Sometimes, in the case of playing piano, the student may fail to bring their hand into a chord position quickly enough. When this happens, instead of just sending a student home for more practice, teachers can diagnose and treat this as a spatial recognition issue and teach the student how to repeatedly put their hand into that chord formation multiple times until that position of the fingers is committed to memory. When a mistake is recurring, it means the body and brain have not learned the shapes and distances of finger sites. This happens not only with piano keys but with finger holes, valve combinations, slide positions, and string-finger positions. And of course, then, the remedy is to use targeted drill aimed at a specific result—not just forced repetition of the specific passage until it sounds correct.

Remedies for Weak Spatial Skills on the Instrument

Here is a very effective exercise to improve spatial intelligence skills for finger positions on an instrument. I call the piano version of this exercise the **Lap-to-*Keyboard* Technique:**

Part One: The student moves the hand or fingers to the targeted note or chord, *without hesitation*.

- The student begins with both hands resting in the lap.
- The student moves one hand to the troublesome chord position and back to the lap.
- The student repeats this exercise until the fingers go directly to the correct keys without finger wobbling or hesitation of any kind. (The brain uses kinesthetic intelligence and spatial intelligence to learn finger placement through a forward and back motion of the hands, *from lap to keyboard*.) Tip for success: Make sure the student keeps touching their lap in between touching the keyboard. This particular tactile effort is important in this drill.

Part Two: The student learns the spatial distance from the preceding notation in the music to the troublesome chord. This is a lateral left-to-right or right-to-left spatial distance *across piano keys*.

- Instead of using the lap as in Part One, the student begins with the hands on the notes that precede the troublesome chord.
- Then the student moves the fingers to the targeted chord.
- This is repeated, again and again, until the keys for the targeted chord can be reached and pressed without hesitation.

- By alternately playing the preceding notation and the targeted chord, the student eventually learns to laterally transition across the keyboard in the tempo of the music.

Here is the **Lap-to-*Instrument* Technique** for woodwind, brass, and string instruments, which begins without tone production:

Part One: The student silently targets the difficult fingering.

- The student removes the hand from the instrument entirely, pats the knee, and then brings it back to the desired fingering.
- By repeating this many times, the student's brain learns to direct the fingers or hand to the correct position on the instrument.

Part Two: The student silently trains the hands to move from the preceding fingering to the targeted fingering.

- The student positions the hands to play the preceding fingering.
- The student then changes the fingering to play the targeted fingering.
- By alternating between the preceding and targeted fingerings, the student learns to execute the changes smoothly, without hesitation.

Part Three: The student tests the results of this exercise by adding sound from the instrument and playing the difficult passage to see if the fingering can be accomplished on time.

(For more detailed instruction on using the **Lap-to-Instrument Technique** see **Addendum 7:** *Classroom Example of Lap-to-Instrument Technic.*)

Other Technical Issues that Require Drill

Another issue that is local to the instrument is being able to play tones quickly and evenly, which can be accomplished through warmups and scale work. Just for fun, my students and I refer to precise mastery of these exercises by an old adage: "One time (playing it perfectly) is *luck*, two times is *coincidence*, and three times is *skill*."

My students appreciate that without complete control of the fingers, their chances of performing with meaning and expression are greatly diminished.

Spatial Transformation from Staff to Instrument

Earlier in this book, we looked at the various forms of spatial *transformation* that occur during a board game—from dice dot shapes, to a numerical system, to the three-dimensional board layout.

Here is an example of spatial transformation in music—the musician has to understand how to adapt information from a vertical five-line staff shape to the particular shape of his or her instrument.

Consider the way a clarinet player reads and plays a three-octave scale. The written version on the music staff for any three-octave scale will show twenty-nine pitches ascending vertically, up the staff lines and spaces in one *continuous straight line*. These twenty-nine pitches also ascend in one *continuous straight line* on the piano keys vertically from left to right. The idea of *one continuous straight line* is a spatial intelligence image.

But tones do not proceed in *one continuous straight line* on the clarinet. The tubing of the clarinet is not long enough. So instead, the scale begins on the lower part of the clarinet cylinder with many holes covered and proceeds upward as fingers are lifted off one by one. This is called the low register of the clarinet. Once all the fingers have been lifted up, there are still more tones to play in order to go higher, so the performer has to use the second register. The tones on the second register begin by covering all the holes once again while using the "register key" (pressed by the left thumb.) As the register key opens, it forces the tones to sound much higher than they sounded on the lower register. The scale continues through the second register by, again lifting the fingers one by one, starting from the lower end of the clarinet's cylinder and proceeding upward toward the mouthpiece. When all the fingers have been lifted for the second time, there are still more tones to play in order to complete the three-octave scale. For the third register, the performer not only presses the register key but also opens one of the holes covered by the left hand, leaving that hole open for all of the third register tones. Therefore, each register (low, middle, and high) began with all holes covered and proceed by lifting fingers one by one in the direction of the mouthpiece. All woodwinds (including flutes, oboes, bassoons, and saxophones) have this type of *tiered system* (or registers) of pitches that creates a much different spatial intelligence image in the mind than the *one continuous straight line* of tones found on the harp, piano, marimba, and xylophone. Brass and string instruments also have similar types of tiered systems of pitches.

The important point I want to make here is that a person who plays multiple instruments—such as clarinet, trumpet, trombone, or guitar—has to possess highly developed spatial transformation skills in order to take notes from the music staff—a continuous, *linear pitch system*—and find those same pitches within a *multi-tiered system*.

Just think how much easier it would be for students in third and fourth grade (who sign up for band or orchestra) to learn about the mechanics and tiered pitch systems of their instrument if they weren't also required to learn new note-reading skills *that they could have learned previously* in PreK through 3rd Grade!

Four Different Types of Transformations

Transformation from staff to instrument is not one skill or one ability alone. Instead, it occurs in four different ways that teachers should become familiar with in order to help students read and perform accurately.

Here are four different ways the brain transforms staff information so it is useable on the musical instrument:

1. **LINKING**—one staff letter on the music staff transformed to mean one place on a keyboard system, fret, finger position, slide position, or valve combination.

2. **PARALLEL MOVEMENT**—translating the *direction* of notes on the staff to the *direction* of finger positions on the instrument. This means musicians using an instrument with a tiered system of pitches must know how to apply information from the music staff to the mechanical tiers of their particular instrument—a type of cognition that requires a little more effort than simply going to the straight line of pitches on a piano keyboard.

3. **SHAPE**—translating the *pattern* created by a group of notes on the staff to the corresponding *pattern* of finger positions on the instrument. For example, translating the pattern line-line-line or space-space-space to the idea of triad and translating the triad on the staff to the corresponding triad made up of finger positions on the instrument.

4. **READING ANGLE**—the ability to take information from a shape or design of notes on the staff *facing one direction* and apply it to an instrument where the tones are produced using a different direction. For instance, reading from a vertical alphabet on the music staff and translating that information to a horizontal alphabet on the piano keyboard (a rare spatial transformation issue that some people find almost impossible to overcome).

One day, an adult student of mine asked why the lesson book couldn't be rotated 90 degrees clockwise so that the *alphabet on the staff* would go horizontally left to right just like the *alphabet on the piano keys*. Obviously, he was bothered by having to transform information from a vertical system on the staff to a horizontal system on the instrument.

The more children master transformative spatial abilities in music, the better equipped they will be for doing operations in math and understanding concepts in many other aspects of the academic curriculum as well. This is discussed in more detail in *Chapter 14: Language, Literacy, and Reading Music*.

The "Backwards" Method for Teaching the Staff

Sometimes a teacher encounters that rare student who does not understand basic abstract principals of the music staff or the alphabet names of the lines and spaces, even after months of instruction. The child might appear very intelligent and very interested in succeeding, but they remain confused when it comes to transformation issues.

These are the students who might benefit from what I call **The Backwards Method**. It's backwards because instead of learning to transform staff information to the instrument, the student learns in reverse—by transforming sounds from the instrument to the staff system of notation. Through this reversed process, they finally understand the correlation that has eluded them.

(For a complete description of this method, see **Addendum 8:** *The Backwards Method*.)

Final Thoughts About Processes in Reading Music

I really believe that every person who can read a book can learn to read music, to some extent. The skills are very similar. But as I have just described, reading notation develops the ability to recognize more than one element at a time (such as pitch and duration) and develops more highly spatial intelligence concepts than reading language.

One can argue that in reading language, words are first recognized through spatial intelligence and then transformed from letter information into thoughts. If the thoughts where immediately typed onto a lettered keyboard, the transformation would be very similar to reading music for an instrument, except that language transformation does not involve steady beat. The use of steady beat all the time in music—for every note in every measure—means that notational reading is a great example of multi-tasking in the brain.

However, when it comes to training the ability to read, we need to learn a great deal from those who teach English literacy. For instance, classroom reading teachers know which students are having problems with prefixes, suffixes, diphthongs, vowels, consonants, etc. When a reading problem is identified in the classroom, these teachers have instructional materials that provide complete lists of prefixes, suffixes, etc. so they can move a student quickly from a reading problem into targeted remedial tasks.

In every grade in school, a child's English literacy skills matter. Teachers never pause to ask themselves how much talent a child has for reading; they simply expect every child to read. And they find the best ways to make that happen.

Chapter 10

Training the Eyes

In *Notational Mode*, just as in reading English, the way students move their eyes can make all the difference. Sluggish eye motion can hold students back and lead to discouragement. Fluid eye motion, especially when purposefully directed, can bring about superior results.

This chapter focuses on the visual skills children need for reading music fluently so that they may perform in a meaningful and expressive manner.

Eye Motion Levels in Reading Music

Five levels of eye motion exist for scanning written notation. These eye motion techniques range from simple to complex.

Level 1: Reading one note at a time—the eyes remain fixed on the symbol being read at any given time.

Level 2: Reading notes in groups or patterns—the eyes move about an inch or two ahead in the music and back. (Notice: this does not refer to memorized note patterns that are recognized in a single glance. Instead, it means recognizing, understanding, and processing all the individual notes in a pattern in a single glance.)

Level 3: Reading two or more measures ahead—the eyes move two to four inches ahead and back in the written music.

Level 4: (Pianists) Reading music for two staves—moving forward on the treble staff, down to the bass staff, and then back up, or vice versa.

Level 5: (Conductors) Reading music for three or more staves—the conductor's eyes mainly go back and forth between looking at the ensemble and looking at the score. As the conductor glances down at the score, the eyes roam freely over multiple lines of written music and are ever-moving.

In all cases where the performer or conductor must look away from the music either at the instrument (such as glancing down at piano keys) or at the performers (while conducting), it is important to be aware that the timing of the glance is crucial. If the glance is too quick, not enough information will be gathered by the eyes. If the glance at the piano keyboard is too long, the performer's eyes may not get back to the page in time for smooth, uninterrupted reading.

Some pianists think they must keep their eyes on their music and are relieved when they are told they may glance down at the keyboard as needed. Sometimes mistakes on the keyboard can be avoided by looking down at the keys just before the hands move a great distance, such as reaching far to the left or right for a final chord.

In any event, when it comes to reading fluidity and accuracy, the eyes play a crucial role in gathering information in time for the brain and body to react.

Improving Eye Motion Abilities

Eye motion techniques for reading do not evolve on their own. Most students will only advance from one level to the next when they are told why eye movement should be improved and then shown how it can be accomplished.

Level 1 visual processing of music notation can be compared to the way children read in the kindergarten classroom—one letter at a time. Most music educators are familiar with the way beginning students are elated just to be able to read one note—any note—on the first page of their new lesson book. Fixed eye motion is normal in the early stages of independent reading. But we should never be so satisfied as to allow a student to stay at that level for long.

When a lesson book indicates that it is time to study whether a melodic interval is stepwise (an interval of a second) or a skip (an interval of a third or more), students should be nudged away from the habit of "see-a-note, play-a-note" and be taught to *compare two notes in sequence.*

This concept can be reinforced by vocal exercises where the instructor points to the notation and the student says "Step" or "Skip" throughout the entire piece of music. Later, the student could identify the sizes of intervals by saying "Second" or "Third." This can be further enhanced by the instructor increasing the speed of the pencil to encourage the student to move their eyes faster.

It's helpful to have the student practice new eye movements by vocalizing without the instrument. This removes the added pressure of using the correct finger positions while trying new eye techniques. That way, all of the student's concentration can be focused on visually and spatially processing note information *on time,* at a faster pace.

Think of how the ability to use advanced eye motion for music notation can lead to greater reading fluency in the academic classroom. Without a doubt, the student who has eye training to look ahead, to read groups of notes, will be better equipped to scan passages written in English.

Once the music student can visually follow the teacher's pencil by identifying the steps and skips in the written music, the student is ready for Level 2 of visual training.

In the academic classroom, Level 2 occurs when children who are usually in kindergarten or first grade read groups of letters in the form of short words such as *cat*, *run*, and *boy*. In second grade, the groups of letters become longer such as *water*, *house*, and *school*.

Similarly, in the music classroom, Level 2 of visual processing involves noticing and identifying small groups or patterns of notes in the music that seem to belong together. It's never about saying, "Read the next three notes in one glance." It's about noticing *why* notes are grouped together. Are they in a group because they contain repeated notes (C-C-C)? Or because they go up or down the scale (C-D-E, E-D-C)? Or because they form triads (C-E-G) or descending triads (G-E-C)?

In this manner, eye motion is connected with *meaning*. It began earlier when the student was asked to identify steps and skip, but now the meaning develops into more complex forms of harmonic rules.

The use of meaning in conjunction with visual music symbols is an excellent preparation for reading comprehension skills in English literacy. In both music and English, understanding that comes by looking at symbols happens at the highest level of cognition in the brain.

Level 3 of visual processing involves reading groups of words (academic reading) or groups of measures (notational reading). Here the eye must travel much farther.

This is where the music instructor frequently reminds the student to "look ahead." This training often begins at one of two different places in the music—on whole notes and when moving from one line to the next.

The student who stares at a whole note while counting each and every beat is often unprepared to play the next note correctly. Instead, we ask the student to begin the whole note and then release the eye so it can roam around, look at the next notes, and then return to finish the whole note (all while still counting "1, 2, 3, 4").

The idea of moving their eyes off any note before the sound of the note is finished makes most students fearful. It means giving up the habit of staring while counting. It's normal for students to harbor a belief that any change in eye motion will destroy their ability to count out the full duration of the notes. That's why it's the teacher's job to instill the confidence that their brains will continue to count any tone without the assistance of the eyes.

Before students can learn to read many notes at once, they have to give themselves permission to release the eyes from staring at the note they are playing.

The type of multitasking I'm describing here is unique to reading music. Reading English doesn't require a person to read a word out loud while simultaneously looking ahead and processing the words that come next. And yet, that is exactly what mature musicians train the eyes and brain to master.

In reading music, the musician processes two types of information at once—pitch and duration. However, the *mature* musician processes not only what is being played, but the information ahead in the next group of notes. We can train anyone to do this by sliding an index card over the note being played so the performer is forced to continue the sound without looking at the note. To most people, this feels immensely annoying because it interrupts the habit they have relied on for so long—staring at the note. But they quickly learn the multitasking skills of reading ahead while also keeping track of the note they are playing.

An Exercise for Better Eye Motion

Here is another simple classroom procedure for teaching students to *release their eyes* from the notes they stare at.

Students can be given a line of whole notes to read from the music staff. They are asked to strike the appropriate bar on a xylophone (or piano key) on beat number one of each whole note, then look up at the ceiling on beats two and three, then return their eyes to the whole note they are playing for beat four. This continues for every whole note in the exercise, without any pauses in the steady beat.

When looking at the ceiling at beats two and three has been mastered, the student can progress to the next step: looking ahead in the music on beats two and three, instead of looking at the ceiling.

Once the music student has confidence that the eyes can roam, the student can be taught to look even farther ahead to scan *groups of tones*.

Reading Groups of Tones

When helping students read music more fluently, the teacher needs to be aware of four different kinds of scanning abilities that are guided by spatial intelligence:

- **Clusters**—scanning notes in groups, usually by step-wise intervals.
- **Changing Direction**—noticing the change in direction and *accurately assessing the number of tones* leading up to and following the change in direction.
- **Skipping**—noticing skips from *line to line* or *space to space* and accurately assessing how long that pattern continues before changing.
- **Neighboring Tones**—recognizing that the next tone in the music is only one down or one up from the current tone.

The first advantage of isolating scanning skills is that it helps us understand the *causes of mistakes*. It's much better for students to be able to overcome a difficulty in a day or a week than asking the student to play a passage or song for an undetermined, unlimited time until the music sounds correct.

The second advantage is that when we accurately identify weak scanning skills, we can subsequently select music that will target and strengthen performance in that weak area.

Here are the scanning skills again, this time with a more complete description.

Clusters. Once the student knows the term *step-wise*, the student is ready to notice *groups* of step-wise tones, such as C-D-E or E-F-G.

Changing Direction. Reading tones that change direction is a local scanning skill at the staff level. First, in order to carry out a change of direction, the student must be able and willing to *make the eyes travel* the entire distance of the ascending or descending passage. And in doing so, must be able to interpret at a glance how many notes ascend or descend. This is essential for speedreading accuracy.

For example, a step-wise passage might ascend five tones, change direction, and descend three tones. The student who hasn't learned to visually process this type of scan will likely guess incorrectly where to change direction. Instead of going up five tones, they may go up only four. However, in my experience, they are more likely to ascend on too many tones rather than too few.

Skipping. Once the student recognizes step-wise progression and clusters, the student is ready to process the idea of *skipping* lines or spaces. This is when the concept of *thirds* can be introduced.

Neighboring Tones. This is the ability to recognize one tone higher or one tone lower than that which is currently being played. Of all the scanning skills, this one really shows the teacher if the student is properly using spatial intelligence to gauge the direction of tones. Unless the student masters this ability, they will have difficulty reading notation accurately.

Fostering Better Reading Methods

In the past, when teachers noticed mistakes in performance, students were told to go home and practice until the music sounded correct. Looking back, that advice seems humorously naïve—as if doing something the same way repeatedly will produce different results. Does hammering away at a musical passage produce better playing? Actually, for some of us, *it did* because that was the only method we had. Back then, old timers referred to this practice as "going to the woodshed"—to do the hard work of learning to play the music on their own.

Today, students can be trained much more efficiently, saving time and effort. By isolating reading issues, explaining them clearly to students, and providing remedial exercises, teachers can make reading music a logical step-by-step process that almost anyone can achieve.

Chapter 11

Alphabetic Logic

Have you ever wondered why some people read music so easily that their hands seem to fly across the piano keys while others struggle just to play the notes? Do some people possess a secret ability that sets them apart from the rest? Are they born smarter or with more musical talent? Or is it possible that hidden traits of "excellence" can be passed along to anyone—and everyone—who reads music?

To explore these ideas, let's look at the way a person learns a new video game. Reading music and operating a video game similarly rely on the rules of cause and effect. When tones descend on the music staff, they also descend on the instrument; when we push a button on the video controls, the action on the video screen changes.

In both cases, the better we are at figuring out the cause-and-effect rules, the more intuitive the rules become and the faster we can play the game and read the music.

What rules in reading music can become so intuitive that the instrumentalist can automatically anticipate where to place the hands next on the instrument? The answer lies in our use of the music alphabet.

Most people *know* the seven letters of the music alphabet, but those who read and play music fluently have a much deeper familiarity with the alphabet than just *knowing* what the letters are. They intuitively know *the order* of the letters. And know it well.

As you'll soon see, the hidden secret that leads to "excellence" is the *fixed order* of the music alphabet.

What is Fixed Order?

To understand fixed order, all we have to do is look at the days of the week. Ask anyone—even a small child—what day comes after Wednesday? They answer quickly and confidently. But if you asked, "What letter is after F in the alphabet?"—the response time is often much slower.

The truth is that many music students *do not consciously use alphabetic order*; yet it is the one built-in feature specifically designed to make reading music *easier and faster*.

In music, our ability to mentally navigate back and forth across the string of fixed letters in the music alphabet is the first part—the conscious part—of Alphabetic Logic. We know we are conscious of the letters because we can mentally "say" them in our mind.

Conversely, we also have spatial and kinesthetic information in the right hemisphere of our brain that we do not talk to ourselves about. We just use the information silently. For example, we can assume that tapping our toe to a steady beat is regulated by the right side of the brain because it occurs without chatter. We never say to ourselves, *Lift the foot up. Place the foot down. Lift the foot up. Place the foot down.* We just do it. We make the foot move to a regular beat. The action requires no language at all. It is managed by spatial and kinesthetic intelligence.

In reading music, we have some activities we can talk to ourselves about and other activities that seem intuitive or automatic. The eventual goal of reading music is to develop reading to the degree that it can be regulated by the right hemisphere and be carried out in a natural, intuitive manner. But the beginning of that process starts in the left hemisphere with a great use of language, as you will see. And one of the strongest elements of language in the beginning stages of note reading is Alphabetic Logic.

In the same way we learn to master the rules of a video game, Alphabetic Logic increases speed by helping the reader anticipate where the fingers and hands will go next.

The originators of music notation built their system of logic upon the fixed order of the alphabet. The letters in the music alphabet never change position. The letter B always follows A. The letter F always follows E. The order is always the same and therefore stable and reliable.

No matter how many times the seven letters of the music alphabet (A to G) are repeated across a piano keyboard, E will be the fifth tone after A. G will be the fifth tone after C. The structure is predictable, reliable, and stable—on both the music staff and the musical instrument.

The Origins of Fixed Alphabetic Order

We can trace the importance of alphabetic order back to the Greeks who gave letters a numerical designation that remained permanent. In Greek thought, alpha meant "the first;" Beta, "the second."

The Greeks attached numerical order to the alphabet, further deepening our ability to "order" information using the alphabet.

On the piano, the fixed alphabet makes hand and finger placement *predictable*. The tone B *always* precedes C. The tone F *always* follows E. The person who is intuitively in sync with these fixed spatial positions finds tones on the instrument quickly through habit and muscle memory. Fixed order makes predictability possible.

Even though the alphabet was added to notational reading as a means of increasing speed, reading mistakes often occur because students disregard the order and logic provided by the music alphabet.

Our Innate Abilities for Alphabetic Logic

Getting back to the question of why some people read easily and other struggle, people seem to be born with natural preferences for how they order information—alphabetically, numerically, by size, etc. Or even whether they put information in order at all. Our preferred method of ordering things can be seen in the way we keep our closets, cupboards, and bookcases.

I estimate that one-third of students *are adept* at alphabetical order. They are the ones most likely to arrange their DVD collection in alphabetical order. Or their guest lists and phone lists in alphabetical order. The alphabet is second nature to them. It's a familiar and useful tool. Cognitively, this may point to higher-order thinking skills for naming (calling objects by the labels "A" or "B"). And it may also point to higher abilities in language intelligence.

Another third of students *have the ability to be adept* at alphabetical order, if they were to train themselves.

The remaining third *have difficulty* using the alphabet at all and compensate by substituting other ways of classifying information in order to achieve success.

I further theorize that students who *are adept* at using the alphabet stand out as "good musicians" and "talented." They sense and anticipate the direction of alphabetic arrangements and move their hands in the correct direction, well before the note has to be played.

Those in the second group who *have the ability* to use the alphabet, learn to read and play music, too, but don't necessarily stand out unless they work very hard to reach that level.

The third group, those who *have difficulty* using the alphabet, shy away from alphabetic tasks. When they learn to read music, they mostly rely on spatial shapes, direction, and distance as much as possible. They play groups of notes well, but they often miss the *starting note* of a passage because it has to be referenced alphabetically.

Alphabetic logic is really an exciting concept for music education because it suggests that students can improve their overall ability in reading music by improving their intuitive alphabetic skills—rather than simply "going to the woodshed" to pound out the notes for hours. This may level the playing field for students who compete for scholarships or chairs in ensembles.

Once a teacher becomes aware that a student is making mistakes due to a weakness in alphabetic reasoning, the teacher can use alphabetic types of drills to quickly strengthen reading skills.

The Role of Alphabetic Logic in Reading Music

Before we look further at the specific ways alphabetic logic is used in reading music, let's understand why the alphabet is used at all. Put yourself in the shoes of the individuals who designed our system of music notation centuries ago.

Their first job was to put something on the page that would refer to a location (pitch) for the voice or instrument. These became the shapes that were written on lines or the spaces between lines. Today they appear as round note heads—some filled black, others filled white.

Their second job was to tell the performer how long to play that sound (rhythm and duration). Those were indicated by whether or not the note head received a stem (an attached vertical line) and any further design added to that stem such as the appearance of attached flags or beams.

This system of note heads and stems provided enough basic information that music could be read using spatial skills, without using the alphabet at all.

To prove this, let's use an example that, on its surface would be highly impractical, yet is nevertheless entirely true. This clearly illustrates how *shapes* are at the core of reading music, not letters.

In this example, let's use the tone known as 440 cycles per second. (This is commonly known as A-440 that orchestras tune to, but in this example, we are leaving out the alphabet letter and just calling it 440 cycles.) We then make up a creative symbol for that tone on paper by drawing a star symbol. For every star written on the page, the saxophonist will play the tone on the horn known as the fingering for 440 cycles per second.

If 440 cycles can be recognized on paper as a star shape, it can equally be recognized by any shape we choose. Let's choose the shape of five parallel horizontal lines with a black dot appearing between the second and third lines (counting upward from the bottom). Every time this dot and line shape appear on the page, the saxophonist treats it exactly as the star shape by playing the tone on the horn known as 440 cycles per second. (Notice that the parallel lines represent the staff lines and the black dot on the second space from the bottom is exactly where we usually read the tone we call "A" on the treble staff.)

We have just created a method using shapes on the staff that have no relation to an alphabet. And yet, it is possible to understand that the black dot on the parallel lines means a particular fingering on the saxophone. It is possible, therefore, to communicate which tone to play on the instrument by using only shapes, without any alphabet at all. And sadly, that's where some of our students remain stuck in their reading abilities when they shy away from using alphabet letters. They are associating a dot on the staff with a fingering. It's very slow, but it's possible.

Instead, it was intended that each alphabet letter would act as handle to pick up the shape information quickly and match it with that same letter on the instrument. Think of a pot on the stove. Most pots have some kind of handle so as to easily pick up the pot. But can we cook in pots if they didn't have handles? Of course. The main function of the pot is to hold the food. The handle only makes it possible to easily move the pot, but we could move it without the handles. In music, we could read the shapes without the alphabet, but the alphabet makes identification and matching with the instrument so much faster.

For us music teachers, the process of checking on students to make sure they are using the alphabet as they read is tedious and feels like a tremendous amount of work—for us and the student. But when we fail to persist in training alphabetic logic, we leave students in the primitive state I just described, void of letters, where all they can do is *guess* using shapes on the staff to match the staff to the instrument.

Ask yourself which labels work best—saying, "I see the icon for 440 cycles per second," or "I see *that thing* on the page," or saying "I see the note 'A'?"

Or while playing a saxophone, "I'm fingering 440 cycles per second." or "I'm using *this* fingering," or "I'm playing the tone for "A"."

The alphabet letter system acts as an efficient shortcut for translating staff locations to the instrument. It takes place this way:

1. First, we cast our eyes on a specific note shape on the staff
2. We remember that note's location as an alphabet letter
3. We seek the matching alphabetic location on the instrument
4. We recall the finger position for that letter
5. We form our fingers and execute the tone for that letter.

Notice that reading music starts with the staff shape and ends with the instrument. Also notice that information goes through a middle process where the staff's alphabet letter is linked to the instrument's alphabet letter.

By identifying these tiny steps, we make it possible to remediate targeted problems within the reading process.

Alternating between Shapes and Letter Names

To be clear, the musician does not rely on alphabet logic or alphabetic identifications one hundred percent of the time in reading music.

Instead, notational reading is based on a toggle system, switching back and forth in the brain between the skill of referencing notes by their alphabet position on the staff and, other times, recognizing shape, distance, and direction.

Toggling is a fluid ability that is *totally controlled by the performer*. In other words, the performer has complete control over where and when shape reading or letter reading will occur. In one instance, a measure could be read just by using letter names. The next time, some or all of the notes could be deciphered according to shape, distance, or direction. Part of the measure could be alphabetic and the other part spatial. It's up to the performer to decide which might work best.

On the cognitive level, reading music reveals a great deal about the brain's instantaneous capacity for making determinations. The choices for how to read notation are determined moment by moment according to a flexible rule system (as if the brain decides over and over, "Is it better to use the alphabet here, or use spatial considerations?"). Or, perhaps more accurately, the brain prefers to read shapes and, as a result, treats shape mode as the default preference, while constantly evaluating where alphabetic information is necessary.

Toggling has great implications for preparing music for performance. Choosing the optimal places in the music ahead of time where alphabetic or spatial skills will be used and then sticking to the plan every time the piece is played might ensure fewer mistakes. Then again, I believe most performers do not need preplanning and rigid adherence to one choice over another because the brain becomes very accustomed to using both alphabetic handles and spatial recognition when needed.

Introducing Alphabetic Scanning Skills

Toggling between reading shapes and using the alphabet is not only the best way to read through a passage of music, but it's also the best way to read and execute *patterns* in the music.

I first became aware of this when I examined the type of mistakes students were habitually making as they read music for the piano. Some mistakes were only spatial scanning mistakes—misjudging the pitch distance between tones, which direction, or the exact staff location. Other mistakes were alphabetic; they occurred as the student improperly judged the fixed order of the alphabet (or did not use it at all).

For example, when a student would come to four ascending step-wise tones but mistakenly play five ascending tones, I recognized that as a *spatial reading mistake*. The error occurred in the recognition of "objects in space." On the other hand, not knowing how to play the *first* tone in the ascending notes would be related to some issue with alphabetic labeling. Either the staff alphabet letter was unknown, the instrument's alphabet location letter was unknown, or both.

Eventually I came to see that there are four basic patterns that commonly occur in music. And there are not only spatial skills involved in interpreting them, but alphabetic skills as well. I call them *alphabetic scanning skills*.

These scanning skills differ from eye motion techniques in that eye motion only describes how far the eye moves ahead in the printed music. Scanning skills use eye motion to find and recognize specific types of information.

The following list describes four common scanning skills the musician must learn to identify and execute. Each of them have a spatial (shape) component as well as an alphabetic component.

Four Alphabetic Scanning Skills

Step-wise—interpreting tones that proceed as line-to-space or space-to-line, going from one alphabet letter to the next. (A to B; or F to G) *Challenge for students: Can the student recite the music alphabet going backwards, one step at a time, as well as forwards?*

Clusters of tones—interpreting groups of step-wise shapes of tones on the staff as *successive* letters in the alphabet rather than reading each tone individually. (Example: Reading step-wise tones as an alphabetic *group* such as D-E-F.) *Challenge: Can the student easily recite three letters of three step-wise tones without pauses or hesitations? In the academic classroom, we would expect that a second-grader would be able to read short words comprised of groups of letters. So too, fluidity in reading music depends on interpreting groups of symbols, shapes, and letters.*

Skipping—interpreting pitch patterns that show notes proceeding upward or downward using every other line or every other space as an alphabetic pattern using *every other* letter, not all letters. (In my classes, we call them line-to-line or space-to-space patterns.) *Challenge: Does the student know the fixed order of the music alphabet so well that the student can recite every other letter?*

Neighboring tones—anticipating the letter below and above the tone that is currently being used. (Example: C-key on the piano is being pressed. The neighboring tones are the D-key [to the right] and B-key [to the left of C].) *Challenge: When the student is shown an alphabet letter, can the student name the letter after and the letter before?*

Adjacency of Letters Within the Fixed Order

You may have noticed that all of these scanning skills are in some way related to the idea of *adjacency*, referring to elements that are next to each other or side-by-side. Our ability to visually recognize adjacency on the staff and replicate it on the instrument are essential for reading music notation. Because the fixed order of the alphabet occurs as a row of letters that do not alter their positions, alphabetic fixed order provides the framework for us to visualize patterns of adjacency. In doing so, we recognize how close the tones are to each other or in which direction they are moving.

Even toddlers can learn alphabetic adjacency when they first learn to arrange alphabet blocks in order. First, the adult would help the child arrange the seven lettered blocks of the music alphabet—A through G—in a row from left to right. Then the child would cover both eyes while the adult removes one block. Finally, the child would survey the remaining blocks to guess which letter was removed. The child who understands fixed order would know F belongs in the empty space between the E and G blocks. This is an easy way to teach the concept of adjacency and develop strong fixed order awareness.

How Alphabetic Adjacency Affects Scanning Skills

Stepwise Movement (or Basic Adjacency)

It is very common for a beginning piano student to identify the piano key "D" yet draw a total blank in naming the next key to the right or the left. That is a clear sign that the student is not referencing fixed order and has not learned adjacency.

Fixed order and adjacency are two principles that could be explored in the general music classroom. Unlike iconic stages, which have little relevance to reading standard notation, helping children learn the fixed order of the music alphabet and games that would teach the concept of adjacency would greatly enhance the ability to read standard notation.

Clustered (Adjacent) Letters

When melody notes proceed in alphabetical order for several or more pitches, students are not using alphabetic logic if they treat each tone as a single entity. Instead, they need to instantly recognize the presence of the fixed alphabetical order within a group or string of notes.

For example, three notes in a measure might be C-D-E, and because the student is not used to looking for groups of adjacent alphabetic letters, the student reads only the C, then figures out D, then moves on to E. I have a six-year-old student who recently learned to read clusters of notes in alphabetic order. This skill has greatly reduced pauses and given her performance a new natural flow.

Skipping (An Advanced Form of Adjacency)

Once a student recognizes adjacency, the next level of logic is to recognize every other letter in the fixed order. This is paramount for spelling triads and working on arpeggiated exercises and passages in the music.

When we encounter students who can never seem to remember the letters in a chord or grasp the concept of line-line-line or space-space-space for building triads, simple written exercises might quickly remedy the situation. Using a blank sheet of paper, the teacher might ask the student to start with the letter A and then write every other letter of the music alphabet. (This would include proceeding past G, on to A, B, etc. so the student has good working knowledge of the *repeating* music alphabet.) The next step would be to write the reverse—the skipping order of letters going backward from G.

Most of us would cringe at putting our students through these types of mental gymnastics. We want music lessons and music classes to be fun. So do children, parents, and school administrators. And yet, we must remember that children have no trouble learning to navigate the days of the week—even backward. It's not that students *can't learn* alphabetic order; it's only that they are *not used to doing so*.

(For a classroom-tested activity on this subject, see **Addendum 9:** *Keep the "Fun" in Learning Alphabetic Adjacency*.)

Neighboring Tones (Adjacency in Both Directions)

To me, this one area of adjacency skills raises a red flag. The inability to use alphabetic *neighboring tones* seems like a *significant lack of alphabetic logic*. The challenge for the teacher is to figure out if these types of repeated mistakes result from a fundamental lack of experience with the fixed order itself, an issue with scanning letters on the music staff, or an alphabetic issue at the instrument level.

I will never forget the day I was teaching a middle school piano student who had just read "C" on the staff and still had his thumb on the C key. Next, he correctly read "B" from the staff, saying it out loud. Then he looked down at the keys, back and forth, left to right, searching for the B-key while his thumb was still on C.

I might have concluded this was a problem that was local to the instrument—that he and I needed to review the names of the piano keys. The C-key should have been a huge clue for locating the B-key—because they are adjacent according to fixed alphabetic order. Then I realized something even deeper. Even though this boy spoke fluent English, he was actually classified as an ESL (ESOL), English as a Second Language student. He and his whole family came from a non-English speaking country. This led me to believe his difficulty with fixed order might be linked to his inexperience with the American alphabet in general.

Other Teaching Tips for Alphabetic Skills

It doesn't take extraordinary effort to improve alphabetic skills. To set the mood for exploring logic and order I ask the students questions such as, "What's the day before Wednesday?" Then, "What's the letter before E?" Or, "What's two letters before G?"

The teacher can also boost alphabetic skills with a simple set of flash cards, each containing one of the seven letters of the music alphabet. Each lettered card acts as a *template for a wide variety of logic questions*. By holding up the card for letter D, the teacher can say "What is the next letter?" or "Name the letter before this one."

Final Thoughts on Alphabetic Logic

The whole topic of alphabetic logic suggests we re-examine how we use the words "talented" and "gifted" in reading music. Are "talented" notational readers the ones who read music well because they score higher on mental acuity tests? Or because they are able to sing and also play "by ear?" Or are they generally conscientious about every subject they study?

Or will we find that "talented" notational readers navigate through their written music more easily because they are adept at using alphabet order?

Hopefully in the future, research will provide clearer insights into these questions.

Chapter 12

Tenets of Linking Mode

This chapter covers one of my favorite topics: *the art of reading music.* Just as people can express their humanity through paint on canvas, through dance, through music composition, through sculpture, through literature—performers can use personal intelligence and music intelligence to shape the sounds on their instrument any way they wish.

That's why students need to be introduced to the art of reading music with musical expression very early—when they first learn simple songs. Once a student becomes aware that they have the capability to play the sound to suit their own personal preferences, the desire for musical expression becomes a powerful motivator for continuing with music.

Technical Accuracy and Musical Expression

Before describing *Linking Mode,* I'd like to discuss some changes that have occurred in music education concerning our attitudes about instrumental technique compared to aural skills and discovery methods.

During my ten years of learning to play the clarinet, I was taught over and over to play the notes accurately, on time, before turning my attentions to style markings, dynamics, and further elements of musical expression. Every band director and instrumental teacher I ever had insisted that I demonstrated my ability to play all the notes at the right time before we worked on any elements of beauty or expression.

This system of instruction produced outstanding musicians and outstanding band and orchestra programs—the kind of ensembles that lifted the human spirit when they performed. A prime example is the college wind ensemble I was fortunate to belong to at Ithaca College for three years—Walter Beeler's Concert Band. During those years, every beginning instrumental student was taught to play technically correct first and then shown how to play expressively. Excellence was synonymous first with instrumental proficiency. But that doesn't mean there was any shortage of musical expression or meaning. Quite the opposite. The ensembles were glorious and inspiring. Every facet of meaning and holistic nuances were present and proudly displayed.

However, in recent times, we see attitudes in music education that are the opposite. For the past two decades, there have been a number of books and articles on music education suggesting that holistic elements in music should actually precede technical instruction and continue through all stages of developing technique. Subsequentially, new methods for reading music have arisen in elementary general music that first delay students from reading music early so they can develop aural skills and then introduces notation through rote learning that develops aural skills more than visual skills.

We need to understand that the rise of these new methods had nothing to do with whether or not instrumental teachers produced excellent musicians. Instead, the concerns were only about beginning bands and orchestras sounding awful, as if students had lost all of their music intelligence sensibilities. (This possibility is discussed in Howard Gardner's chapter on Music Intelligence.)

On the surface, the idea to make early note reading experiences more musically meaningful makes perfect sense—until you notice the results of these efforts. Because general music classes have only focused on natural music abilities (such as imitation and rote learning) without developing any spatial intelligence skills required for reading notation, most children in elementary grades are unable to read any notation in their general music song books unless they've had private music instruction.

Although I don't recommend adding music intelligence skills into intital decoding stages, I do recommend combining aural memory with decoding as soon as the student can play the piece accurately to a steady beat. This process is not new. Every instrumental teacher who has helped young students develop into mature musicians has taught accuracy in decoding first before coaching the student in musical expression. And that's why instrumental methods consistently produce the excellent musicians who sit in our professional bands and orchestras—these musicians were taught the holistic elements of musicianship after their technical skills were intact.

Combining elements of holistic musical expression with accurate decoding is the advanced process I referred to previously as the third mode or *Linking Mode*.

If we are someday going to establish notational reading programs in early grades in school, we need to understand how this mode works so we can help children transform their mechanical-sounding decoding abilities into the *art* of reading music.

The following outline suggests which intelligences are used in Linking Mode.

> **Note to Reader:** You'll find coded letters next to the activities to indicate the particular intelligence used. As explained before, this list doesn't mean I am excluding the presence of other intelligences or other factors, but merely pointing out which intelligences have the *greatest* influence and benefit.

Table of Codes for Intelligences in Linking Mode

K=Kinesthetic, **L**=Language, **LM**=Logical-Math
M=Music, **P**=Personal,
SP-r =Spatial Recognition, **SP-t** = Spatial Transformation

The Order of Tasks in Linking Mode

This is the three-step process our brains use to combine our music intelligence knowledge with the skills of decoding:

1. **Recognition:** Using *auditory skills* **(M)**, the performer first uses *Linking Mode* to hear and recognize the particular style or type of music being decoded, at that moment in *Notational Mode* **(SP-r, K)**. For example, *recognizing* that the music being performed is in jazz style, not other styles such as Baroque or Classical.

2. **Selection:** Second, once the brain can recognize the type of music being played, the performer uses *Linking Mode* to retrieve similar information from *aural memory* **(M)**. For instance, *Linking Mode* can locate and bring forward the characteristics of jazz from aural memory that were acquired through listening and experiencing jazz.

3. **Application:** The performer references the samples brought from aural memory **(M)** and compares them to the sounds he or she is producing on the instrument at that moment **(SP-r, K)**. We might say then the performer *mimics* certain aspects of the selected aural memories, such as duration, dynamics, and energy flow **(M)**. For example, the performer might remember how duplets (two eighth notes) sound in jazz style (the first tone in the duplet is lengthened, the second tone is shortened). The performer uses "remembered jazz-style" to shape the manner of the duplets being played in real time. (Jazz duplets are different from traditional style duplets which are played "as written," where each tone in the duplet is given almost equal value.) **(Aural, notational, and interpretive skills combined: K, L, M, LM, P, SP-r, SP-t)**

And *voila!* We now have the reasons why music develops the whole child—all major intelligences are engaged at once in *Linking Mode*. This means *every* intelligence is active in *every* measure of music played when applying musical style, expression, or meaning to reading skills.

Another way of looking at it is that *Linking Mode* combines the musical intelligence information located on the short neural pathways near the cortical input (where aural information enters the brain) with knowledge of abstractions and symbolism on the longest neural pathways in the deepest part of the brain, at the fifth tier of cognition. It also makes use of personal intelligence as the student chooses which type of sounds to apply and which to ignore. And of course, kinesthetic intelligence is used in the physical operation of the instrument.

Since I know of no other subject that makes such full use of multiple intelligences, it's my opinion that music activities in *Linking Mode* surely must have the greatest potential for cognitive development in children.

Interpretive Practices in Classrooms

Using music intelligence while reading notes is not automatic and rarely develops on its own. I have met teachers and students who, sadly, seemed totally unaware of interpretive ability and were not knowledgeable in the area of musical expression. For them, the main focus in reading music was technical accuracy. They operated solely in *Notational Mode*.

Therefore, we can't assume that all people who read music have the instrumental skills or the cognitive abilities to play music with expression as it was originally intended by the composer.

That's why we all need to understand the methods and procedures for learning to use *Linking Mode* so that we can effectively guide children in this wonderful ability to make music meaningful.

My Personal Quest for the Secrets of Musical Expression

When I played clarinet in high school, my teacher encouraged me to play, as he said, "with *love*." He didn't realize it, but that was his attempt at shifting me into *Linking Mode*. However, it didn't work because I was deficient in stored *aural references*. Thankfully, I was able to remedy this at Ithaca College, where I was required to attend every concert and recital given on campus for four years. These experiences built a tremendous collection of aural sound bites.

Similar to my experiences, most young performers are still in the process of building their cognitive library of aural references. However, a lack of aural experiences should never stop any student from learning interpretive aspects of music. Interpretive skills can be mechanically stimulated through direct teaching—which I also received at Ithaca. My professors taught me step-by-step the weight and length of sounds and how energy flows through the music.

In that manner, I learned to bring music to life through *my teachers'* aural experiences. They described music as *they* had experienced it. Through their descriptions, I became more aware of what to listen for in audio examples as well as in the music I performed.

It was the combination of building aural references on my own *and* acquiring directly taught techniques that combined to develop my interpretive playing. Throughout my life, the ability to play interpretively has given me a great deal of satisfaction and pleasure. That's why one of my missions as a music educator is to promote opportunities for students to learn interpretive skills early in life. Certainly, students seeking these skills should not have to wait, as I did, until they are in college!

We shouldn't assume, either, that developing natural abilities in music will automatically prepare a student to play expressively. Prior to playing clarinet, I grew up in a family and community that routinely sang in four-part harmony. We sang around the piano whenever visitors came to the house. We sang at church and community events. I sang a solo in church when I was four and learned to sing alto parts when I was eight. I belonged to all my high school vocal groups and directed the youth choir at my church. I had extensive experience developing my natural aural music abilities.

Yet, clearly, my ability to sing did not help me play expressively on clarinet. I was probably so locked in to mastering my spatial and technical abilities on clarinet that including musical expression required targeted guidance and training.

Today, I provide students with interpretive examples within the first three months of instruction, starting with how to emphasize the primary beat in the measure. When eighth notes are introduced in the lesson book, I show them how to "add weight" to the downbeats and "lift" the upbeats.

When I prepared piano students for formal classical recitals in New York City, I made great use of language examples (such as "tu-na fish" for two sixteenths and an eighth note) when my students needed to replicate nuances and inflections in the music. Language examples not only improved my students' abilities for that moment, but seemed to be easily absorbed into their permanent aural memory for subsequent performances.

Here is an overview of the different ways *Linking Mode* occurs, followed by specific classroom examples.

Applications of Linking Mode

In my experience, our ability to combine natural and structured music knowledge through the third mode can occur in any of the following four ways:

- **Natural Application**—Being able to apply characteristics of *Aural Mode* to notational reading with little or no training (rare).

- **Assimilation**—Learning to use interpretive applications in small steps over time to let the aural senses guide notational performance.

- **Split Focus**—A self-directed method of *willing the mind* to immediately operate in *Linking Mode*.

- **Comparison**—Using knowledge from aural memory while reading music, to judge technical note accuracy and aural expression in music *being performed by others*. (A skill used by teachers and conductors.)

Examples of Interpretive Learning

Let's look at those four applications again through some of my classroom experiences.

Natural Application
First, I think that naturally occurring musical expression is rare. I have never seen someone pick up a musical instrument, read notation for the first time, and play in a relaxed, beautiful style right away. That doesn't mean it can't happen. I just haven't seen it.

However, I do remember one of my students who significantly improved with very little coaxing. I consider him my best example of *nearly* natural interpretive abilities.

Every Saturday, this young boy attended my piano class for four- and five-year-olds. He always came to lessons with his head held high, sporting a big smile. His mother seemed very proud that her son loved music so much.

After this child attended my class for four or five weeks, we finally reached the page in his book containing his favorite song, "Twinkle, Twinkle Little Star." Just before this particular lesson began, his mother had told me her son had spent the entire week learning how to read and play every note. He was very eager to show me his progress.

I watched him play the first two notes—C, C. Then I saw his eyes move to the next pitches. They were Gs. He performed the Gs correctly. Next, he had to read two As, which required moving his pinky finger beyond the regular hand position. I held my breath as he continued, silently rooting for his success. He completed the song—*reading* and playing all the pitches.

His performance had been awkward and full of pauses. Nevertheless, I placed a sticker on his page. I was pleased that he had pushed himself to *read* all the pitches—not just avoid the work of reading by playing the song "by ear." I was particularly pleased that he had completed his performance without giving in to his habit of stopping to chat with me.

Then, I tried an experiment. "Let's play the song one more time," I told him. "But this time I want to you to play it the way you sing it. Okay?" He agreed.

He started in again. I leaned down close to his ear and joined him, quietly singing the song as he played the notes. This time, he didn't sound awkward. I backed off and allowed him to continue without my voice leading him. He finished the whole song, pressing the keys in time to the "singing" in his mind. What a difference from the first performance!

For me, this had been a spontaneous experiment. I had no idea if my suggestion would work. Yet, it turned out to be an *Aha!* moment. I knew what I had witnessed was a young child's ability to combine personal aural memory with notational reading.

Assimilation
As seen in the last example, interpretive performances are easier to achieve when the student is playing a song he or she knows well. Yet, the purpose of reading instruction is to teach students to read so well they can read unfamiliar music. Learning to play unfamiliar music interpretively is a reading habit that takes years of training and practice. It is the teacher's job to help the student *assimilate* interpretive examples into the music

lessons until the student is capable of using personal aural memory all the time.

A good example of assimilation happened when I taught Shawna, an adult student, to play the first page of Beethoven's *Fur Elise* during her piano lesson.

Over several weeks, Shawna had learned all the correct notes in the first section. But the music still sounded choppy, stiff, and mechanical.

To help her add grace and beauty to the beginning passages, I sang the melody, emphasizing the weight and length of the notes. This, however, did not help her improve.

So then, we discussed how her fingers should strike the notes alternately between heavy and light. That suggestion didn't work, either.

We talked about downbeats and upbeats. No improvement.

Finally, I thought of my own playing and how I feel when I put my hands on the piano keys to play *Fur Elise*. To me, the opening measures of the song felt similar to the sensation of placing my hands in soft bread dough as I pushed my fingers down into the dough and pulled them back up. Down, then up.

When I motioned with my hands and explained this bread dough metaphor, her face brightened. I could tell that Shawna related to my words because of her own experiences kneading dough.

She brought her hands to the keyboard once more, recreating the "bread dough" feelings in her hands as she pressed the piano keys, pushing, then pulling all the little notes.

The results were magical. I told her it sounded as light and flowing as if Beethoven himself were playing.

This shows how important it is for music teachers to believe in the process of assimilation and *persist* until the student is able to transform mechanical, technically correct playing into graceful, interesting music.

Split Focus

Here is a completely different way of teaching interpretive skills. I learned this method many years ago while helping a snare drummer prepare for solo competition. He was the kind of student any teacher would spend more time training. He had such a great attitude about music, and he didn't mind putting in all the effort necessary to reach the level of excellence.

We were working after school in the band room. He seemed very prepared, note-wise. His rudiments were cleanly executed. But that afternoon, he could not play the solo all the way through. I asked him to slow down. I tried to get him to concentrate. Nothing was working. He was too nervous and kept making unexpected mistakes.

Sometimes, as a teacher, you just *know* things. I could see, if he continued to be this nervous, he was not going to do well at the competition.

Finally, out of desperation, I said, "Let's try something new. Pretend you are two different people. One person is operating the sticks. The other part of you is in the back of the auditorium at the controls, adjusting the way the music sounds."

He began again. This time his sticks hit the drum head and didn't stop until the whole solo was complete.

"Perfect!" I said. "How did you do that? You even surprised me!"

We tried it again. And once more, it was perfect.

Through the years, I have used split focus with many instrumental students. As long as they can accurately play all the notes first, this method consistently works well. For many years, I had no idea why. Now I think it's because split focus helps a student access their aural instincts to guide their instrumental technique—by using *Linking Mode*.

An added benefit of split focus is the way it squashes the tendency to be nervous. Perhaps this is because, in *Linking Mode*, all the intelligences are at work simultaneously. No major part of the brain is left idle so it can act out common nervous behaviors like talking to one's self, shaking, sweating, having breathing problems, or blurred vision.

Comparison
A person who is teaching or conducting also uses the third mode, but they use it in a different way. Instead of improving their own personal performance, they are judging the performance of others in order to help them improve.

This happens when the teacher or conductor uses their spatial intelligence to read printed music while aurally listening to an ensemble or soloist perform. As the director listens, he or she uses *Linking Mode* to compare the sounds of the performance to his or her own *stored aural memories*. Then the director makes informed judgements about which aspects of the performance will have to change in order to match the director's recollection of the way the printed music should sound.

In this case, instead of the performer using stored memory and making the changes, the teacher or conductor uses *their* stored memory and requests the changes.

Final Thoughts on Linking Mode

Believing that *Linking Mode* exists and articulating how it may work are only the first steps in understanding this complex process.

It's my hope that science, medical, and educational research will verify and expand the description I've presented in this chapter.

The reason I am confident that we do, indeed, have a *Linking Mode* is the fact that this model matches everything I've learned about teaching the expressive qualities of music. I see no gaps or areas that can't be explained when music activities are viewed through the *Aural*, *Notational*, and *Linking Modes*.

Chapter 13

Chronic Mistakes Syndrome

The discovery of the third mode—*Linking Mode*—opens the door to solutions in music education that were not previously available, as you will learn in the following example.

Battling The Elusive Demon

Some well-trained pianists easily perform in public in a variety of settings, be it their church, the concert stage, or assisting in rehearsals. But there are other pianists who are just as well-trained who unfortunately find it very difficult to perform in public at all. They get nervous, their hands shake, and their eyes fail to read the notes properly whenever they are under pressure to perform well.

Because they studied and worked just as hard as good performers, the people who have difficulty performing wonder why they are less capable. They don't understand what's interrupting their ability to perform, so they silently blame themselves—for not being smart enough, talented enough, or for not working longer hours to perfect their music.

What they don't realize is that all these symptoms are not their fault. They're just caught up in a small destructive habit—one that can easily be fixed.

Some people call it "the nerves."

I call it Chronic Mistakes Syndrome.

Why Is It Called A Syndrome?

A syndrome is a condition characterized by a related set of symptoms.

Here are the Chronic Mistakes symptoms that appear suddenly, during music performance, regardless of past ability to play those notes correctly:

1. "Blanking out"—the performer realizes the images are music notes but, for that brief moment, can't associate the shapes of the notes with the correct letter names or key locations.

2. "Leaving notes out"— the performer realizes his or her eyes skipped over some notes, usually in the beginning of a measure.

3. "Giving the wrong letter name"—the performer misreads the location of a note, for example, thinking the note is on the second space when it's really on the third.

4. "Correct letter name, but wrong piano key"—the performer knows the name of the note but fails to strike the correct key on the piano.

Another way to identify this syndrome is by the fact that the errors are, indeed, random and never predictable. They are the opposite of skill-based errors such as an inability to reach a chord on time, inability to play scale passages up to speed, or inability to play arpeggiated passages. Skill-based errors occur every time, *in the same place in the music*, until the performer works out the problem. Instead, with Chronic Mistakes Syndrome, accidental errors *come as a complete surprise*, in measures that were previously played "perfectly."

The Cause Of This Syndrome

This syndrome is caused by an imbalance between aural abilities and spatial abilities while using *Linking Mode*. Here is how it happens:

The performer decides to work on a piece of music. It might be two or three pages long. The performer learns to play the entire piece and has confidence that every note is correct, even though there are occasional pauses here and there each time.

When it comes time to perform in public, the performer's first measure is flawless, while using all of the spatial intelligence skills required for *Notational Mode*. Every note is read correctly from the staff and accurately played on the instrument.

Two or three measures into the piece, the performer begins **transforming** the notes by adding expressive qualities in the melody. Being a well-trained musician, the performer finds it easy and enjoyable to push the melody to greater heights with subtle changes in dynamics and slight alterations in tempo.

In that instance, instead of staying in *Linking Mode*, which combines aural and notational skills, the performer wanders from partially using expression while recognizing shape, distance, and direction to complete reliance on natural abilities, music intelligence, and playing notes "by ear."

At first, the performer is not aware that his mind has departed from reading the written music even though his eyes are still staring at the correct measures on the page. At that point, he is totally playing "by ear." Suddenly he runs out of improvised notes and needs to find what's next in the written music. Here is where panic sets in. Even if his eyes are looking at the correct notes, it takes a second to switch out of natural abilities back to using spatial intelligence to decipher notation. Being able to accurately read, in that instance, is as difficult as regaining one's place in a written speech after extemporaneously going off course.

The performer may struggle to keep the music on the steady beat. Or the performer's fingers reach for the correct keys but end up on the wrong keys. He is almost offended by how wrong the mistakes sound. Now rattled, he forces himself to use his spatial skills in *Notational Mode* but it's no longer the calm, controlled spatial process he began with. He fears making the next mistake, but he will continue the destructive pattern over and over. Throughout the beautiful piece of music, he will continue to randomly switch in and out of natural and formal abilities, trying to be expressive, yet fearing technical imperfections.

A person with chronic mistakes syndrome has a great desire to perform well. That's why he or she diligently over-practices every piece of music, trying to eradicate every error. Unfortunately, this extra effort causes more harm than good. The more familiar the music becomes, the greater the chance that the aesthetic characteristics of the melody will distract from correct notational performance. The person hears where the melody is about to go and senses how it is about to rise and fall. Soon fingers ramble on, playing small parts of the remembered melody without looking at every single note on the page.

What I'm describing is a process in which spatial skills are momentarily dropped in favor of total immersion in musical expression. When the performer drops using spatial intelligence to read the music, the performer loses his place in the music. And shortly after, loses confidence.

In *Linking Mode*, there has to be a balance between the use of spatial abilities and music intelligence. Both have to be present; at no time can the reader drop spatial skills for reading to wander off into the la-la land of expressive abilities. Allowing music intelligence to take over completely is a formula for disaster.

What is *The Scatter Technique*?

Fortunately, I've discovered a very effective remedy for Chronic Mistakes Syndrome. It's called *The Scatter Technique*.

To use this method, the performer practices reading measures on the page in random order. That way there is no continuous, holistic melody line to draw the performer away from spatial skills. Using random order, the performer learns what it feels like to concentrate on spatial skills in every measure. This greatly improves note accuracy. Reading random measures will feel different as the eyes and brain become skillful at identifying every note without skipping or guessing.

Within a month or two of using this technique, reading skills become significantly stronger. Then the musician can go back to applying the aural refinements of *Linking Mode* because the spatial skills will not be dropped. The performance will be balanced, containing both spatial abilities and music intelligence all the way through. Confidence to perform in public can be established and maintained.

How to Use *The Scatter Technique*

Step 1: The musician chooses a slow enough tempo that would allow accuracy in the most difficult measure of the piece. That becomes the tempo throughout *The Scatter Technique* for that piece of music.

Step 2: The musician selects a measure near the bottom of the first page of the piece. (The exercise will remain on this page during this practice session.) He or she plays only that one measure and stops, making sure every note was played accurately while keeping a steady beat.

Step 3: The musician selects other random measures anywhere on that same page, playing slowly and accurately. Because these measures are selected at random, *there is no melody line to lure the reader away from spatial reading skills.* This allows the musician to stay in *Notational Mode*, focusing on spatial reading skills and complete accuracy.

Playing random measures will feel strange, at first. The musician's mind may rebel and say the exercise is too hard—but that's the point. The very reason this syndrome exists is because the spatial reading synapses are too weak. Corrective measures always require extra effort. The more the musician practices *The Scatter Technique*, the stronger the synapses, and the easier it will be to read every single note, without fail—even later when musical expression is reintroduced into the performance.

Step 4: This step sounds daunting but it's central to eliminating Chronic Mistake Syndrome. The musician connects random measures, one after the other, as if they were one long continuous made-up song.

The tempo must be very slow to give the eyes time to scan and read properly. As the musician completes the first random measure, he or she scans the page for another measure. Without stopping the beat, the musician proceeds from the first measure into as many random measures as possible.

The better the ability to read across the page in a random fashion, the stronger the ability to avoid accidental mistakes.

Step 5: After practicing random measures for fifteen or twenty minutes, strictly in *Notational Mode*, the musician can return to the beginning of the piece to try playing the measures in melodic order. Then aural senses can once again embellish the treatment of the melody and harmony lines—hopefully, with improved spatial reading skills and much fewer mistakes.

One final comment: I believe that Chronic Mistakes Syndrome is a condition that will reappear from time to time, whenever spatial skills have once again fallen dormant or need reinforcement. We learn from neurobiology that synapses weaken and strengthen according to use. The musician should never be discouraged if a tendency for accidental mistakes does reoccur—especially when *The Scatter Technique* can restore those skills so easily.

Variations of *The Scatter Technique*

After mastering random measures, the musician can expand *The Scatter Technique* in two ways that will offer greater challenges and higher rewards.

- **Two Measures in Succession**. Instead of choosing single measures on the page, the musician chooses groups of two consecutive measures, then switches to a different set of two consecutive measures. Sometimes this is easier because the eyes don't have to jump to a new random place as often.

- **Toggling Between Two Complex Measures**. Sometimes when proceeding from one measure to another random measure, it occurs to the performer that the transition could have been better. Or the notes in the random measure could have been played with more authority or accuracy. When this happens, the musician can attempt a second try by returning to the previous measure to toggle back and forth between the old measure and the new one, until both measures are satisfactory. Then, without stopping the beat, the musician can move on to random measures again.

The Scatter Technique can also be referred to as *Spatial Longevity Training* because it helps the performer concentrate on correct spatial reading for much longer, without errors.

Long Term Effects of Chronic Mistakes Syndrome

Chronic Mistakes Syndrome is a symptom of weak spatial skills in the presence of very strong aural skills. When musicians are skilled at playing "by ear," it becomes easy to "fake" notes they don't feel are important to read spatially. It's as if they abandon interpretive and notational skills for a moment to totally bask in playing "by ear," which is *Aural Mode*.

This *unplanned* switching back and forth from notational-interpretive skills to aural skills that causes so many mistakes doesn't just affect one performance, or even a few. It eventually erodes a musician's sense of competency and thereafter stymies all desire to perform in public.

How Well Does *The Scatter Technique* Work?

I have personally used *The Scatter Technique* to keep myself from falling into this syndrome. I've shared it with my students, as well. I've shared my ideas with other accomplished musicians who have admitted that they, too, have experienced the woes of mentally wandering from the written music.

The Scatter Technique offers new hope to reluctant performers. It's a consistent plan for accuracy that leads to satisfying results.

Chapter 14

Language, Literacy, And Reading Music

Spatial intelligence is the common denominator that links reading music to academic learning in reading, math, spelling, and many more subject areas.

It's logical to assume that as spatial skills are developed through reading music, children's spatial skills for reading words are strengthened, as well. Likewise, as spatial skills in academics improve, the child is better equipped to read music.

I believe that is why music teachers used to wait until students reached the end of the kindergarten year to let them enroll in private music lessons. By then, the academic teachers had trained the students to spatially recognize many different shapes. And through reading readiness activities in PreK and kindergarten, such as learning to cut and paste, children had developed spatial and kinesthetic skills.

Now we know that music teachers are equally as capable of developing children's spatial and kinesthetic neural pathways in PreK and kindergarten through Companion Words, early student xylophone programs, and activity centers for reading notation.

Reading Words

Children begin the process of reading words by sharpening their spatial intelligence skills. In PreK, they learn to recognize the shapes of circles, squares, rectangles, and triangles. This helps them recognize the shapes of individual alphabet letters and numbers. Later, they recognize groups of letters and numbers.

We don't usually think of letters and numbers as shapes. But it is easy to see these skills from the point of view of the child if you compare the difference in shape between "t" (t) and double "t" (tt). The shapes t and tt look different. In order to pass spelling tests, students have to recognize these small details.

Unfortunately, in education, we often want to rescue children from the work and frustration of having to spell correctly, in favor of creating a free environment for learning. We think that lifting restrictions will boost their creative writing. Indeed, it may—initially. But when we fail to ask the child to go back to the essay, as step two in the process, to spell words correctly, what we are really doing is failing to train student's *spatial recognition abilities* for noticing punctuation, capital letters, and the construction of sentences and paragraphs.

This second step in the process can easily be explained to children as a change of hats. When they are creating, they wear their imaginary "free expression" hat. Then, *just as professional writers*, after creating they go back and look at their work again while wearing their "fix-it" hat. By learning to isolate and improve these two processes, children maintain a strong feeling of free expression while at the same time developing an appreciation for polishing their work.

Abstractions in Reading

Along with developing spatial intelligence in early reading, children must also begin using simple abstract reasoning. They are able to do this even though they are still physically developing their prefrontal cortex. It helps students if music teachers and classroom teachers exercise extra patience while waiting for children to mature enough to understand our adult abstract terms.

Some of the abstract concepts children will encounter in academic reading are:

- vowels (a-e-i-o and u)
- consonants (b-c-d-f-g etc.)
- prefixes (a group of letters in front of a word, such as "re"- for rerun)
- suffixes (a group of letters at the end of a word, such as "-ing" for running),
- diphthongs (combination of two vowels that together make one sound as "ie" in the word "believe.")

Eye Techniques in Reading

The greatest factor that enables children to proceed from reading single letters to grouped letters is the development of their eye motion skills. It's not just a matter of scanning more letters at once. In concert with eye motion, the brain learns to distinguish *groups* of letters within the whole word (examples: *read*ing, re*print*, un*end*ing).

Similarly, students who read music must also use special eye techniques to see small divisions of the whole beat, such as eighth notes, triplets, and sixteenth notes. Otherwise, when they see a measure with many small notes, they become confused and can't recognize where the beats occur in the measure.

To remedy any confusion, I teach children to "circle the beats." Using a pencil, they circle any note or groups of notes that comprise a beat. In a 4/4 measure, there would be four circles. (Examples: the first circle might contain an eighth note and eighth rest. The second circle might contain two eighth notes, etc.)

Drawing the circles with a pencil trains the eye to eventually "see" the circled groups of notes automatically when entering new measures. After students learn to physically circle the beats, I train them to "circle the beats" in their mind alone.

Similarly, in the academic classroom, eye motion also plays a large role in the child's ability to read words in a book in a steady, flowing manner. At first, the way students read books out loud sounds similar to the way beginning instrumental students read music for the first time. The reading is choppy as their eyes only take in small amounts of information. There are gaps between words in early word reading—the same as there are gaps between sounds in early notational reading in band or orchestra.

The job of the academic reading teacher, as well as the music teacher, is to provide enough practice and encouragement for the student to relax the eyes in order to scan larger amounts of information at one time.

This scanning ability, whether used for words or notes, plays an important role in absorbing content and meaning from what is being read. In word reading, the child must learn to do more than just say the words, but also listen to how the words are grouped in order to recognize their meaning.

Meaning in music is also dependent upon scanning ability. Once groups of notes can be read and then produced on the instrument, without faltering, the student can sense the rise and fall of phrases in the music. These musical phrases sound very similar to our sentences and phrases in our spoken language.

Whether reading words or notes—accuracy and technical ability precede content meaning.

Giving Children Time to Grow

No matter which kind of reading a student engages in, for music or words, the student must physically build and strengthen undeveloped neural pathways. Consistent daily practice will strengthen and lengthen the neural synapses until they become securely established. Students in the regular classroom study reading every day, and students are encouraged to read books at home all during the week. So, too, band and orchestra students are encouraged to practice daily.

This is why reading standard music notation requires a long-range plan from PreK on—the same as reading words in the academic classroom. Reading doesn't happen overnight. Or in a week or a month. The changes that need to be brought about in the brain require years of development.

Because note reading and word reading are so similar in their use of spatial intelligence—they perfectly complement and reinforce each other. The more children read music notation, the easier it is for them to read words. The better their visual and spatial skills in the academic classroom, the better equipped they are to read music.

Omitting Spatial Intelligence Training

One of the greatest travesties in American education has been the relaxation or omission of spatial intelligence skills needed for reading and other subjects. We have gradually placed less emphasis on spelling requirements, handwriting exercises, representational drawing exercises, and music reading. These all would develop the student's ability to recognize shape, distance and direction—spatial skills necessary in every aspect of visual learning.

Other Language Arts

When writing essays, book reports, and fictional stories the content is guided primarily by language intelligence. But *formatting* is guided by spatial intelligence.

When students review their written work, before handing it in, they use spatial intelligence to scan every sentence, making sure each begins with a capital letter (large shape) and ends with a period (a small dot shape). They must learn to indent the first sentence of every paragraph, a task that requires shape recognition and location of letters.

These academic examples can be compared to a type of formatting that occurs on the music staff. Music students use spatial recognition to *align* written numerical counts beneath music notation. As rhythms become more complex, the accuracy of this *visual alignment* becomes more critical for playing the rhythms correctly. Hence, a student who is used to the detailed process of aligning their written counts under music notes is better prepared to align indentations and margins in language arts.

Another academic example of using spatial intelligence is our use of paragraphs. Often, in my own writing, I try to break up my chapters into the smallest paragraphs possible, indenting often. This, I feel, helps the reader better understand my topic and avoid getting weary as they plod through long, run-on paragraphs. In a similar manner, my editor is always curbing my run-on sentences and encouraging me to break them into smaller segments. These considerations would not be possible without spatial intelligence alerting me to the size and shape of paragraphs and sentences.

Also, in editing written compositions, spatial intelligence assists in the location of thoughts. When the writer decides a sentence in the middle or end of a paragraph should be moved up to become the lead sentence, that is a decision based on location—a feature of spatial intelligence.

In metered poetry, the creation of a steady pulse is guided by spatial intelligence (measuring regular distances) while the meaning and choice of words is guided by language and personal intelligences.

Also in poetry, music intelligence helps the poet hear and feel the sound and flow of the words to the beat.

In free form poetry, the shape and length of the lines are decided through both personal intelligence (personal choices) and spatial intelligence (using shape and distance considerations).

In haiku, spatial intelligence guides the shape of the lines while language intelligence supplies the words and meaning.

In all of these poetry examples, words are chosen according to the duration of syllables as well as the inflection. Duration is a feature of spatial recognition in terms of distance through time. We sometimes decide whether to keep or replace words based on the length of their sounds.

Math And Spatial Intelligence

Two ways in which spatial intelligence helps student in math is through written calculations and math word problems.

Math Calculations and Music

Depending on the method used, for written calculations, the student must place numbers in their proper positions on the page. For instance, when multiplying a three-digit number by a two-digit number, the student will write the three-digit number directly above the two-digit number, as if they are in a right-justified stack. Then a line is drawn beneath the stack, and the answers will be written beneath that line. What I have just described requires spatial intelligence to align the numbers correctly before any calculations have even begun.

To carry out the multiplication, the student must then use spatial intelligence to select the digit on the lower right to multiply each digit in the number written above.

Spatial intelligence also helps the student locate the proper place to write the answer—below the line. Often there are reasons why answers and parts of answers have to be *indented from the right*. This indentation is difficult for students to remember at first until they have repeated the multiplication process many times.

Students in third and fourth grade who have difficulties in multiplication and division are not necessarily weak in math skills or understanding mathematical concepts. They might be weak in spatial intelligence—knowing *where* to write numbers during math calculations. The remedy is to provide worksheets that test and train *spatial locations of objects* until the student shows sufficient improvement.

If all students were well-trained to "recognize objects in space," think how that would boost their performance in math.

Similarly, the general music classroom is a perfect training ground for spatial location skills. I used to hand out 8" x 11" laminated sheets of yellow construction paper on which I had drawn a large version of the treble staff. Because the image of the staff was large, I could see everyone's card positioned flat on their desk as I walked around the room. The students would move a colored plastic disk, the size of a poker chip, up and down the staff lines, matching whatever directions I sang to them. "Place your note on the first line . . . move it to the third line . . . fourth line, fifth line . . . first line again." We would practice on the spaces, too.

In this manner a class of twenty-eight students learned the spatial names and locations of the lines and spaces, as well as their alphabetic names—all in a few moments of what appeared to be a game.

Math Word Problems and Music

Besides improving a student's ability to perform math calculations, spatial intelligence is necessary for math word problems. *If a train is traveling at 30 miles per hour, how far will it travel in 4 hours?* The student must spatially understand segments of distance along the train track and then add them or multiply them. Without spatial reasoning, math problems do not make sense to the student at all. That is why many math teachers use manipulatives such as cubes, blocks, or other tangible objects that the student can see and touch to build experience in spatial intelligence.

How Reading Affects the Broader Curriculum

We sometimes forget how vital reading is to other areas of the curriculum. The student who has trouble reading will be at a disadvantage learning any subject in the social and physical sciences.

The best way to give every child a fair chance to succeed in every subject in school is to see that there is optimal brain development during the formative years, as soon as the child enters school.

A Personal Story About Spatial Training

Sometimes books are born from an author's trials in life. *The Neuroscience of Reading Music* did not begin in that manner. I simply decided to write what I'd learned about music with no thought of my own personal history.

However, about halfway through the writing process, I remembered some events in my own childhood that closely aligned with this topic of spatial intelligence and academics.

At age five, when I first entered school, my rural school district did not offer kindergarten, so I went straight into first grade. I was the youngest child in the class. The top third of my classmates were students who were not only a year or two older than I was but also repeating the grade. Compared to all the other children, I was very immature. Throughout my elementary school years, it was difficult for me to learn at the same rate as other children.

In those days, good grades were marked on our report cards with blue or black ink. Failing grades were marked with red ink. My report cards were filled with "red marks." At the end of each grading period, students with red marks did not receive their report cards directly from the teacher as the other students did. Instead, they were required to pick up their report cards at the principal's office by standing in a long humiliating line of students in the hallway. After waiting for our turn, we'd enter the principal's office and nervously inch closer to his desk as he sorted through all the report cards. When he got to mine, he'd open it, stare at it for a while, and then sternly ask, "Why did this happen?"

Can you imagine how hot and sweaty I felt during the long silence that followed? I had no idea how to answer his question.

But that was only the beginning. When I took my report card home to my parents, Dad's response was far more thunderous.

Failing grades defined my elementary school experience. I was often kept indoors at recess to catch up on backlogged work. By the end of seventh grade, the teachers requested that I repeat the grade so that I would be better prepared for secondary education. My father emphatically refused.

In eighth grade, something even more horrible happened in our family. My mother contracted a serious illness that confined her to bed. This meant that, in addition to attending school, I had to take over the housekeeping, cooking, and childcare for my younger brother and sister. But that didn't stop me from wanting music lessons. I begged my father to let me use his old clarinet that was stored up in the attic.

After Christmas, despite the extra housework, I began clarinet lessons at school. I remember sitting for hours in front of a Rubank Elementary Method clarinet book, playing whole notes and learning to count. The first month seemed difficult, even frustrating. But I persisted. Four months later, my music teacher told me I had progressed so much that I was ready to join the high school band.

None of this made my mother happy. She worried I might fail the New York State Regents exams in June, and subsequently, fail the grade.

But that never happened. To everyone's amazement (even mine), I passed the Math Regents with a score of 98 percent. In addition, I passed all the other Regents exams, as well. At eighth grade graduation, I was called up to the podium to receive two academic awards—one for math and another for social studies.

No one had expected me to ever succeed academically! Looking back, I can see why it happened. Not only was I very young for the grade level, but there were no music or art classes in my school that would have increased spatial intelligence abilities needed for reading and math. By taking clarinet lessons, I had to visually recognize music symbols, transform information from the music staff to the instrument, and learn to play to a steady beat. No doubt all of these music reading skills strengthened my neural pathways for spatial intelligence information.

I still remember that first day in band—forcing my eyes to follow the notes in the music. My eyes couldn't make it to the bottom of the page without getting lost. On subsequent tries, my eye movements and scanning abilities increased. Soon, I did learn to easily keep up.

After eighth grade, I became an average and above-average student. There were no more trips to the principal's office. I enrolled in all the Regents classes, performed in all the high school music ensembles, and even became president of my class. In my senior year, I was accepted to Ithaca College School of Music in Ithaca, New York.

I believe that learning to read music opened up a world of new possibilities for me and for my family. Now I wonder how many of my fellow students who stood with me in those long report card lines simply lacked better eye motion techniques and spatial intelligence abilities.

We can't change the past. But going forward, we can improve education for others.

New Aural Trends About to Impact Secondary Ensembles

Now that you have a clear understanding of what notational reading is and my personal story of how it may have improved my own academic abilities, you may understand why I grow increasingly concerned about national efforts in music education to alter the curriculum for instrumental ensembles at the secondary level. There is a growing movement to add aural learning to band and orchestra classes so that students can better interpret and understand music.

I have no objections to secondary students learning to interpret and understand music. We can establish special classes for that, if necessary. But, in my opinion, reducing any time from notational reading to allocate towards the study of aural skills is not the way to support our students' spatial reading skills or cognitive abilities—not in elementary or secondary education.

In addition, by adding new aural requirements to our secondary ensembles, we will hamper every director's ability to focus on the technical skills students need to read and perform at their highest ability. Any reduction in valuable rehearsal time risks producing weaker performances and possibly less community support, which eventually could result in reduced funding for music.

Chapter 15

Effective Notational Reading Programs

In school music programs grades PreK through 12, instruction for reading music can help less-fortunate students overcome socio-economic barriers by opening the door to music scholarships, teaching careers, and opportunities to compose or conduct. It's the low-income students who rely on music instruction in school when they can't afford private music lessons. Sometimes a student's family does not have the educational background or financial ability to support their musical gifts, so their best hope for comprehensive music training is in public schools.

Providing instruction for reading music during the school day may greatly enhance spatial intelligence skills that will affect English literacy, math, and all other subjects that require reading and writing.

While it's easy for us to talk about equal opportunities for all students, implementing the necessary changes to bring about those opportunities requires targeted guidance that, hopefully, would come from experienced educators who have already developed successful note-reading programs.

In that regard, the rest of this chapter contains my suggestions and comments intended to help set up and maintain early reading programs.

Sometimes setting up a new program is not just about getting the details right but also convincing others that the changes are both necessary and workable. (To this end, I again refer you to **Addendum 3:** *Aural Myths in General Music*.)

Bear in mind that the plans described here are for PreK through 3rd grade, but they could just as well be applied to a grade higher, as a K-4th grade program.

Practical Considerations for Establishing a Notational Music Program

For children to develop independent, fluid reading skills, and for those skills to become established by the 3rd grade, students need practice in reading from the lower portion of the staff, then the middle, then the upper portion. Ideally, this would include eleven pitches on the treble staff, beginning with C_4 (Middle C, below the staff) up to F_5 (the top line). We have already established that these spatial reading skills have to be learned in a particular order and mastered so they can become stable. By my estimation, this requires a carefully administered five-year program from PreK through 3rd grade.

In a home-school situation wherein there are only a few of the same students, this would be easy to achieve over a five-year period. But in public and private schools where class enrollment is much larger, the following issues must be considered:

1. The balance between time allotted for aural skills and time for notational skills.

    a. Keeping notational training to a minimum so there is time for aural skills

    b. Choosing the most effective methods so students learn quickly and retain the information

2. The changing enrollment. Every time a class of twenty-eight students graduates from one grade level to the next, the names on the class roster change. Some students move away; some students

are held back; some students enroll for the first time. As the roster changes, how can the lessons always remain "kid-friendly" and accessible to everyone? How can everyone feel successful at every grade level?

The solution to these issues lies in our ability to manage how and when the eleven pitches of the treble clef are studied. A general music teacher might choose a plan where students learn to read three pitches in PreK and Kindergarten (C_4-D_4-E_4), then expand reading to five pitches (C_4-D_4-E_4-F_4-G_4) in first grade, then have students read eight pitches for the C scale in second grade (C_4-D_4-E_4-F_4-G_4-A_4-B_4-C_5), then add the remaining upper pitches in third grade (D_4, E_4, F_4). In other words, the range of pitches in songs could increase from three to eleven. In the earlier grades, students could read five-pitch nursery songs such as *Mary Had a Little Lamb* or the chorus of *Jingle Bells*. In the second and third grade, they could read songs with a greater range such as *Yankee Doodle* or *Row, Row, Row Your Boat* among other songs from their general music text books.

However, I believe this kind of plan would only be *partially* successful and perhaps might cause more harm than good if songs with a range as great as eight tones were so ambitious that it turned some students off of reading music at all.

While a few students might learn to read and play a large range of pitches (from C below the treble staff to the top F line), the majority of the class would not—especially if time segments for teaching notation were kept to a minimum in order to keep up with singing, improvising, evaluating, and all the other important aspects of music. Children can get discouraged and give up if they fall behind the achievement level of the class. As the number of pitches greatly increases, I believe some students would stop trying altogether.

Is our goal in public school classes to have children demonstrate advanced note reading abilities, or is our goal to develop basic reading skills along with the spatial reading abilities that improve cognition? If it is the latter, we can better accomplish that by using *small* pitch ranges each year—

small enough that the average student will enjoy note reading and the below-average reader will not be left behind.

To this end, I propose a **Three-Five Pitch Plan** where *most* students would achieve a good measure of success each school year—even if they enrolled in that particular school late, in second or third grade.

In the Three-Five Pitch Plan, the teacher requires the mastery of no more than three or five pitches for each year.

The plan would look like this:

- Learn the Lower Treble Staff—Key of C
  - In PreK with 3 pitches (C_4-D_4-E_4)
  - In Kindergarten with 5 pitches (C_4-D_4-E_4-F_4-G_4)
- Learn the Middle Treble Staff—Key of G
  - In 1st Grade with 3 pitches (G_4-A_4-B_4)
  - In 2nd Grade with 5 pitches (G_4-A_4-B_4-C_5-D_5)
- Learn the Upper Treble Staff—Key of a-minor.
  - In 3rd Grade with five pitches (A_4-B_4-C_5-D_5-E_5) plus F_5 (the top line of the treble staff)

Note to Reader: The number after each alphabet letter in the outline above indicates the exact location of the pitch on a piano keyboard according to American Standard Pitch Notation (ASPN). Personally, I do not recommend announcing this numbering system to young children, although it can be very useful after third grade.

Each octave of pitches on a keyboard receives its own number designation. The first C on the left side of an 88-key piano keyboard is called C_1. The letters that follow, going to the right, are D_1-E_1-F_1-G_1-A_1-B_1. The next key is C_2, followed by D_2-E_2-F_2-G_2-A_2-B_2. The next key is C_3, followed by letters with the code number 3. And so forth.

> Middle C is always C_4. When there are seven Cs on the keyboard, the last C to the right is C_8.
>
> On an electronic keyboard, there are fewer keys. Then you would first label Middle C as C_4. The Cs to the left of Middle C will be C_3 and C_2. The Cs to the right will be C_5 and C_6. In this manner, the cycles per second of C_4 on a keyboard will match C_4 on any piano. In this manner, the keyboard numbering system will be perfectly aligned with the piano.

The Importance of Review During Each Year

When students are in 1st and 2nd grades and learning the middle of the staff, the teacher should *occasionally* go back and review pitches from the lower staff that were learned in PreK and Kindergarten. The review works best by beginning slowly with three-tone songs, then over a few weeks graduating to five-tone songs. If these review sessions are kept short, even new students who were not in the notational program in PreK and Kindergarten can catch up with the class on previously learned pitches.

Sight Reading in Early Grades

One more concept that teachers must remember when teaching children to read in early grades is to provide lots of sightreading exercises and songs that include unfamiliar patterns. So often we can fool ourselves into thinking students are good readers when they may actually be demonstrating their ability to play or sing songs from memory. A little memorization is okay during the reading program—we want children to enjoy the songs and have a sense of pride at their accomplishments, even if their songs are memorized. But the teacher who is determined to teach children to read independently will also include many unfamiliar examples *until children are fluent readers.*

Music Dictation is Useful at Any Level

Throughout any successful reading program for music, reading skills are greatly enhanced with the addition of aural and written activities. I recommend music dictation as a very effective aural and notational method for teaching rhythm and, sometimes, pitch. In this activity, children experience the sound first and then transcribe it into notation. This corresponds to #4 of Howard Gardner's description of spatial intelligence: the ability to produce a "graphic likeness of spatial information." The child visually recognizes distance and direction of clapped sounds and then uses spatial transformation to write the information in the form of music notation.

But dictation is only effective when using simple rhythms first and building the hierarchy over time. Remember the need for hierarchy in the building and establishing of the long neurons that extend deep into the brain. We start with simple concepts and move to the complex because that is how the neurons develop—from simple to complex.

Once familiar with the procedures for dictation, children can take ownership of the process, administering dictation to each other or to the class instead of always having the teacher direct the learning.

Here is an example of how children might administer music dictation to each other. The children sit on the floor or at tables in groups of two, facing each other. One takes on the role of "teacher;" the other, "student." The "teacher" performs a four-beat pattern of quarter notes and rests on a rhythm instrument while the "student" uses a pencil to write the appropriate number of "sticks" and "squiggles" on a blank paper fastened to a clipboard. After one example of dictation is concluded, the two children switch roles. They keep performing and writing dictation, taking turns until they hear the ringing of the music teacher's bell. This signals all the children in the room to scramble to find a new partner. The teacher redistributes the clipboards to each "teacher-student" group and dictation continues.

Music dictation can also include pitch by using tone blocks (one xylophone bar attached to a block of wood). The child who is writing the sounds records the rhythm (sticks and squiggles). But this time, the student adds an alphabet letter for pitch beneath each "stick." This works best for children when pitches are limited to three tones in alphabetic order.

It doesn't matter if the room becomes a little noisy with the excited voices of children at play.

Later, when the students are seated quietly, the teacher can administer the dictation for all the children to write, simultaneously. Then, it's important for the teacher to provide immediate feedback of the correct answer. This reinforces the students' correct "guesses" and builds confidence. If the rhythm or pitch examples are simple enough, they will fit into the children's hierarchy of understanding and most "guesses" will be accurate.

Music dictation is always a powerful means of deepening the understanding of symbolism, regardless of the student's age.

Lesson Ideas for The Three-Five Pitch Plan

It's one thing to say what *should be* learned and another to decide actual lesson plans at each grade level. Here in this section are some suggestions for implementing note-reading activities. Some ideas have come directly from my own classrooms, and some are just ideas that I believe would work based on my experience teaching at each level. Regardless, I hope that these suggestions spur on each teacher's own creative ideas for effective note reading strategies.

Notational Strategies for PreK

In PreK, the first three pitches of C-D-E can be introduced through the Companion Words story while in morning circle. Children can also become familiar with the shapes of music notes by engaging in cut-and-paste activities with whole notes, half notes, and quarter notes—the same way they learn geometric shapes for reading words.

In addition, children of this age enjoy reading from large cards containing quarter notes and quarter rests in a four-beat pattern. The children clap the notes saying "quarter" and put their finger to their mouth, making a "Shh" sound for the rests.

After they are familiar with these four-beat patterns, children enjoy rearranging the order of the symbols. They can sit in groups of two and "play teacher" by asking their friend to clap and say the pattern they choose. They can roam the room, visiting learning centers stationed around the room set up ahead of time by the teacher. At these learning centers, children read from different patterns of C-D-E from poster cards and perform those tone patterns on various instruments. Here they would learn to differentiate between the high and low characteristics of the pitches. They could practice sequential order of shapes *and* sounds with graduated tone blocks, then with tone bells.

Notational Strategies for Kindergarten

In kindergarten, children would expand their three-note knowledge of C-D-E (learned in preschool) to C-D-E-F-G. This would easily be accomplished by continuing the Companion Words story, first by sitting in a circle while discussing the story and then through learning centers providing experience on instruments similar to those just described for PreK.

In addition, the concept of staff lines could be introduced in kindergarten using only one line at first, teaching students to make an X mark "on the line," "below the line," and "above the line."

Students in kindergarten could learn the concept of spaces by being presented with a large sized G-clef staff along with four crayons: yellow, blue, red, and green. The students would color each of the spaces all the way from left to right with any color they choose as long as each space is a different color. Then the teacher would give each student some objects (dried beans or corn, paper clips, squares of cardboard, etc.) and give directions such as, "Place a dried bean on your red space," or "Place a paper clip on your yellow space." Because understanding the spaces is abstract, this will help the children "see" the space in the future.

Notational Strategies for First and Second Grades

To be efficient, a comprehensive program for reading music should be presented as a *spiral curriculum*. Therefore, by using the kindergarten year as a model, the plan can be repeated for the next three years in first, second, and third grades, gradually increasing children's ability to read level one and level two rhythms.

First and second grades could concentrate on the middle of the music staff since the lower staff, C-D-E-F-G, has already been explored in PreK and kindergarten. Now reading will concentrate on the tones G-A-B for first grade and G-A-B-C-D for second grade.

By just concentrating on G-A-B in first grade, students who might previously have been overwhelmed with the five pitches in kindergarten will find the switch back to only three tones a refreshing change. It would be a fresh start at reading from the staff. And now that they are older and more mature, they might be better able to spatially recognize locations on the staff. I regard first grade as the year in which independent note-reading can really be established in many students. With only three tones, and with children's prior experience for two years, first grade can be the year that children read tones more fluently.

First graders would repeat all the activities experienced in kindergarten music—still using student xylophones, learning centers, compositions, and composer examples—but do all of that using the new tones on the middle of the staff for G-A-B. (It would also be good to review songs using C-D-E from previous years.)

First grade students are capable of making up simple compositions with three pitches in the following ways:

- by writing their "songs" using three letters G, A, and B, known at first as Low, Middle, High.
- by making up their own iconic symbols for their own compositions using these three pitches
- by using just two staff lines to record Low (G line), Middle (A space) and High (B line) instead of working with all five lines of the staff.

The reward for writing compositions in music class is the joy of watching others perform them. By sitting cross-legged on the floor, facing each other in pairs—students can take turns playing "composer" and "performer." The composer hands the performer a written composition. The performer attempts to play the written music on a rhythm instrument or student xylophone. The composer learns to listen patiently and, at the end, offer constructive comments.

In later grades, these types of compositions can evolve into scores for small group ensembles in music class that can even be performed at parent-teacher meetings.

In my experience, original compositions are always well received by the community. And students take great care to play the compositions in the exact manner required.

Students also enjoy taking their written compositions home to their families as *tangible* accomplishments to "show off" what they learned in music class. When students compare music class to academics, they sometimes conclude that "music doesn't matter as much." Students, their parents, and administrators need visual evidence that music instruction is improving their lives in a personal, meaningful way. *Their written compositions instill a greater respect for their own music accomplishments* as well as appreciation for composers of all genres.

Second graders would repeat the same types of activities as in first grade (using student xylophones to read notation, exploring in learning centers, and composing), but this time the number of tones would increase from three to five: G-A-B-C-D. Even though these tones put songs into the key of G with an F#, this new group of tones, G-A-B-C-D, does not use a sharp. This means that the idea of keys, sharps, and flats can be postponed until after third grade when students might be using a keyboard—where sharps and flats can be visualized on the black keys. For second grade in public and private schools, the focus should still be learning the names of the lines and spaces on the treble staff, not learning to read and play in different keys. When teaching large groups of students at once, it's better to do a superlative job teaching a limited subject than to miss the mark trying to cover too many topics in too little time.

By second grade, students should already be very familiar with level one rhythms (signifying one beat or greater than one beat) and would move on the level two rhythms where the beat is divided.

Here students can first learn the sound of eight notes that appear as duplets through the use of language. By using the words "slow" for a quarter note and "quick-quick" for a duplet, eighth notes that occur in pairs can easily be read accurately. Passages of music can be read out loud using "Slow, quick-quick, etc." until the teacher is convinced the student is translating the notation properly. Once the student understands that eighth notes must be played faster, the idea of the downbeat and upbeat can be demonstrated. Here is where the loop counting system becomes very practical and effective in note reading.

(Again, for a detailed explanation of this counting method, see **Addendum 4:** *The Loop System of Counting*.)

Notational Strategies for Third Grade

Third graders would need a lot of review. They would need songs using C-D-E-F-G and G-A-B-C-D, learned in previous years. Then for new material, they would go on to use the highest area of the G clef by learning songs in a-minor on tones A-B-C-D-E (and F). This would introduce the concept of Major and minor tonalities.

The great advantage of using the a-minor scale is the opportunity to introduce third graders to simple songs in a-minor. After four years of music instruction in PreK, K, 1st, and 2nd grades, third graders will welcome moving past songs that have become "ho-hum" to something new and exciting. Not only are minor keys good for spooky sounding songs for Halloween, but some of the happy-sounding Jewish songs for Hannukah are also written in minor. The change to minor keys will help third graders take pride in their new higher level of music achievement.

Another exciting change for third graders is the introduction of triplets and sixteenth notes. But I would hold off on introducing combinations of eighths with sixteenths or introducing ties and dotted quarter notes until older grades. It would be better to focus on the ability to read fluently from any area of the staff than to get bogged down with new, complex counting ideas at this grade level. The idea is to *establish* reading from the staff, and this requires a great deal of repetition of letter names on the staff to build those long neurons that travel to the deepest part of the brain.

In third grade, recorders might replace xylophones. Learning centers and composing would still be very effective.

Because this plan establishes the *basic* elements of reading music by the end of third grade, students would be fully prepared to take private music lessons or sign up for instrumental electives in school. With a complete knowledge of the staff by third grade, general music students in upper elementary grades could move on to *full-sized keyboards, guitars, and full-sized standard percussion instruments.* They could fully develop their compositional skills through MIDI keyboards and even prepare for jobs in the music industry.

A music program that trains both aural and notational skills trains every student to reach their full potential, not only in music, but in life—because it builds the type of brain that can learn almost anything.

Nothing Happens Without Steady Beat

As a reminder, no plan for implementing new and better programs for reading standard music notation in schools will be complete or fully effective without first establishing the most basic element of music—steady beat and whole body coordination.

If we are really serious about helping every child reach their optimum ability to learn and function in the school environment, we must start in PreK with this fundamental physical attribute that tunes up a child's ability to read, spell, and understand math. As discussed earlier in Chapter 4, educator and researcher Phyllis Weikart set the groundwork for developing whole-body coordination and steady-beat skills.

In an ideal learning environment, every child entering school would be tested for the ability to walk to the steady beat of an audio signal, including their ability to swing their arms as they walk (in the opposite direction of their foot movements). And then PreK and Kindergarten classes would offer plenty of the Weikart activities and exercises until all or most children demonstrate whole-body coordination.

We, as a society, have been willing to increase children's learning abilities by offering them breakfast programs. It's time to boost learning again by utilizing Weikart's research to implement lessons that will develop children's bodies and minds so they can learn more and learn faster.

This book has outlined successful notational reading programs that will build and strengthen spatial and kinesthetic synapses. Add to that whole-body coordination for every child and we will see every aspect of learning flourishing as never before.

At least that way, we will know in the end that we did everything we could to give our children the brightest future possible.

Chapter 16

Notational Reading Goals for Music Literacy

Beyond a five-year startup plan for learning to read notation, we should also be looking at elementary grades from a top-down view listing all the notational reading goals we think are important.

The goals in the following list could be spread out over seven years (PreK through 5th grade) or spread out over ten years (PreK through 8th grade).

This outline could serve as a start-up guide for establishing music literacy in any public or private school. It could also serve as a resource for writing national goals for establishing visual skills for music literacy.

Foundational Skills for Music Literacy
PreK through 5th (or 8th) Grade

1. *Steady Beat Proficiency*

Ability to walk, swinging arms in opposite direction to feet

Ability to walk eight steps forward to audio beat

Ability to walk forward eight, back eight to audio beat

2. *Deciphering Notation*

Ability to name rhythm symbols
  Level 1: One beat and greater
  Level 2: Divisions of the beat
  Level 3: Cut time, 6/8 simple and compound time

Ability to name music markings
  Format markings (measure, bar line, repeat signs, etc.)
  Dynamic markings
  Style markings

Ability to identify each of the following:
  Lines and spaces of the Treble Clef
  Intervals
  Sharps, flats, naturals
  Time signatures
  Key signatures
  Ascending and descending notation

3. *Reading Fluency*

Ability to read and perform:
  Steps
  Clusters of tones
  Skips
  Neighboring Tones

Ability to sight read short passages

Ability to read tones on
  Lower portion of treble staff
  Middle of treble staff
  Higher portion of treble staff

Ability to sightread
  Level 1 rhythms
  Level 2 rhythms

4. *Instrumental Proficiency*

Student xylophones
- Proper use of mallet
- Ability to play music to a steady beat
- Ability to strike keys to play songs when reading alphabet letters
- Ability to strike keys to play songs when reading from Treble Staff
- Ability to perform alone and in groups

Recorders
- Ability to produce characteristic tone
- Ability to play music to a steady beat
- Ability to learn finger positions
- Ability to play passages from alphabet letters
- Ability to play passages from the music staff
- Ability to perform alone and in small groups

Piano Keyboards
- Ability to identify each of the following:
- Patterns of black keys
- Middle C (C_4)
- Sharp, flat, and natural keys
- Octaves, intervals, skips, scale-wise
- Ability to demonstrate:
- Finger Warmups
- Scales
- Chord and chord exercises
- Ability to play music to a steady beat
- Ability to read and play simple songs from Treble clef
- (Advanced) Read and play songs from Bass clef
- Ability to perform alone and in groups

5. Graphic Representation

Ability to draw all music symbols appropriate for that grade level

Ability to take dictation using symbols appropriate for that grade level

Ability to compose written rhythmic patterns and rhythmic compositions

Ability to compose written pitch patterns and compositions on music staff

6. Interpretive Reading Performance

Ability to emphasize primary and secondary beats

Ability to lengthen or shorten tones for effect

Ability to speed up or slow down the beat

Ability to transform piece into different moods

Ability to play written music in the manner in which it would be sung

Chapter 17

Future Research In Music

Today in education, we need the kind of research that measures the effectiveness of a particular skill set in music instead of using broad, vague labels such as "those who participated in music."

We want to know the specific *type* of participation—whether the performers are playing instruments "by ear" (Aural Mode) or by reading standard music notation (Notational Mode). And someday, we may even be able to measure whether participants are using these modes alone or using Linking Mode (combining aural and notational abilities).

The following are examples of the types of research we need in order to understand the ways music activities and curriculum impact student learning and behaviors.

Ten Topics for Study

1. Which group of skills most consistently raises academic scores—aural, notational, or a combination of both?

    The word *both* could apply to the middle school student who spends most of jazz class improvising (Aural Mode), then attends band class later in the day reading music (Notational and Linking Mode). Or another student who goes to African drumming class during school (improvising in Aural Mode) and takes piano lessons after school (Notational and Linking Mode).

2. Compare the reading and math progress of children who participate in a five-year program reading standard music notation from PreK with children who receive no training in standard music notation from PreK through 3rd grade.

3. Discover if the ability to read standard music notation is a factor in whether a student completes high school or drops out. Also, is it a factor in whether or not a student seeks further education after high school?

4. What percentage of 6th grade students who attend general music classes for seven years or more—who *did not* learn to read standard notation through a music elective or private music lessons—are able to fulfill basic music literacy requirements such as the ability to select and read five random pitches on the treble staff?

5. How many children in Grades 3-8 who sing from general music books can correctly sight-read any two consecutive measures of music notation in the general music book they have been using?

6. What are the factors that cause one student to practice lesson assignments daily and another student to practice sporadically? Is the greatest influence the teacher, the parent, genetic makeup, friends, the number of after-school activities, desire for achievement, or a natural tendency to establish good habits in other areas of life?

7. What kind of instrumental music lesson assignments raise *reading ability* more quickly—

   - A balanced plan of technique, reading, and performance?
   - More technical exercises and less reading in a method book?
   - More reading in a method book and less working on technique?

- Or more performance music than method books, including more of any type of music the student wants to study?

8. Which raises note-reading ability more quickly—

    - practicing random measures (spatial training)?
    - doubling practice time?
    - or using flash cards that train alphabetic logic (fixed order)?

9. Using electronic imaging, what are the differences in the brain between reading words and decoding music notation (while making sure they are both executed without vocal or musical expression)? How do they differ when both words and music notation are processed while incorporating expressive elements?

    How does the electronic imaging differ when the student reads words with expression compared to without? Similarly, does electronic imaging differ when the student reads and performs expressively from standard notation compared to merely decoding without expression?

10. Using electronic imaging, what does the brain look like when a child associates a pattern of visual symbols in 6/8 time (such as standard notation for the title of the familiar nursery rhyme "Humpty Dumpty") with the memory of what that pattern sounds like compared to the brain of another child who is shown the same pattern of standard notation in 6/8 time and is able to decode all the individual symbols in the pattern? In both cases, what does the imaging show about the use of short neurons for aural processing and long neurons for visual-reading skills while the child is processing the information?

I hope these suggestions have stimulated your own curiosity and perhaps inspired you to test your own assumptions through research.

Chapter 18

The Promise of Tomorrow

Many people have confided in me about their regrets at never having learned to read music. Some grew up thinking that reading music was too difficult; others believed it was too late to learn. Most of them regarded those who could read music as very intelligent, extremely talented, or just lucky. In every case, I felt sorry that they never discovered how capable they probably were and that they never experienced the joy I've known from reading and playing my favorite music.

That's part of the reason I believe we have an obligation to make reading music easier and more accessible. Everyone deserves the opportunity to be musically literate, to examine the great musical works that have been collected over the centuries, and to write their own compositions.

Getting to know a composer up close by *reading and performing* their manuscripts is a much more in-depth experience than sitting in an audience where music passes by in an instant and disappears. We may not all have the ability to improvise or to play long pieces by memory, but most people who read music can find written examples of their favorite music in books or online, at an easy-enough reading level to enjoy playing them.

Reading music enables a person to belong to a large ensemble—such as a band, an orchestra, a community or church choir—to perform great ensemble literature, and to learn the give-and-take of ensemble teamwork.

There have been instances where the ability to read music elevated someone from the lower echelons of poverty to a lucrative career in the music industry, thereby changing the whole trajectory of their life.

And perhaps the biggest reason for reading music has nothing to do with music at all. Notational reading can improve cognitive growth, and especially spatial intelligence abilities, for all age groups.

If we truly want excellence in our schools, children can no longer afford to wait four to six years from their entry into school to be introduced to standard music notation. Students need the visual eye techniques and spatial/kinesthetic training from reading music that builds the neural pathways for spatial intelligence and provides a jump-start on cognitive excellence in *both music and academics.*

It's not so much a question of *when* young children are ready to read music. It's a matter of choosing the most appropriate learning strategies for their age level.

Howard Gardner said it best in *Frames of Mind:*

> "What research has shown, virtually incontrovertibly, is that whatever differences may initially appear, early intervention and consistent training can play a decisive role in determining the individual's ultimate level of performance. If a particular behavior is considered important by a culture, if considerable resources are devoted to it, if the individual himself is motivated to achieve in that area, and if proper means of crystallizing and learning are made available, nearly every normal individual can attain impressive competence in an intellectual or a symbolic domain."
>
> —H. G.

ADDENDUMS

Addendum 1

Guide to Understanding the 2015 Amherst Study

TITLE OF THE STUDY: Taylor, P. et al. The global landscape of cognition: hierarchical aggregation as an organizational principle of human cortical networks and functions. Sci. Rep. 5, 18112; doi: 10.1038/srep18112 (2015).

You can find this as an open access document at: https://www.nature.com/articles/srep18112#Abs1

You would want to look for words in the study that relate to music skills. You will find them near the end of the article in the pyramid diagram marked Figure 10:

1. at the highest tier of the pyramid (the longest neural pathways)
2. at the lowest tier of the pyramid (the shortest neural pathways)

First, scroll down to the part of the document that is labeled DISCUSSION.

Find Figure 10, the large diagram in the shape of a pyramid. Note that beneath the pyramid diagram, they describe the diagram as an "over simplified graphical model." Right away I noticed that the words on the first tier of the pyramid generalize the skills that were measured rather than list the individual skills. This generalization leaves out the music skills. To see the music skills, you must scroll down halfway into the paragraph beneath the pyramid diagram where you see the following:

> "At the sensory end of our lists, emerged tangible language-related behavioral elements such as: prosodic, speech execution, musical cognition, whistling, auditory discrimination, music comprehension/production, pitch, prosody, musical tones, auditory perception."

Notice that these are natural music abilities related to music intelligence. The sensory end means closest to the sensory inputs, using the shortest neural pathways.

The next sentence describes the fifth and highest tier reached by the longest neural pathways.

> "At the abstract end emerged features which at face-value appear similar to the preceding list, though perhaps vary in degree of symbolic content: naming, braille reading, word generation, word stem completion, phonological discrimination, phonology, readers, orthographic, languages, lexical, semantic, names, identity."

While the authors of this study were not looking at skills related to reading music, these skills at the fifth tier are undeniably associated with the decoding and interpretation of written symbols—all written symbols—which could just as easily be music symbols as alphabet letters or numbers. Hopefully in the near future, similar studies will measure the location and function of music intelligence skills compared to notational reading skills. In addition, we need studies that measure pure decoding of music symbols compared to decoding with musical expression.

Addendum 2

National Music Goals in Relation to Reading Music

This is an excerpt from the website www.nafme.org/my-classroom/standards/ that explains the 2014 National Music Standards. Although it uses the word "literacy," the excerpt doesn't mention reading music at all:

> **"The 2014 Music Standards are all about *Music Literacy*.** The standards emphasize conceptual understanding in areas that reflect the actual processes in which musicians engage. The standards cultivate a student's ability to carry out the three Artistic Processes* of
>
> - Creating,
> - Performing, and
> - Responding.
>
> These are the processes that musicians have followed for generations, even as they connect through music to their selves and their societies. And isn't competence in Creating, Performing, and Responding what we really want for our students?

Students need to have experience in creating, to be successful musicians and to be successful 21ˢᵗ century citizens.

Students need to perform—as singers, as instrumentalists, and in their lives and careers.

Students need to respond to music, as well as to their culture, their community, and their colleagues."

—2014 National Music Standards, nafme.org

In my opinion, we can't have music standards that are "all about literacy" without teaching children to read music. Again, notice that reading music is not one of the goals.

One could say that reading skills are *implied* here because a person can create, perform, and respond through music notation. But the opposite is also true. It's possible for children to create, perform, and respond to music on a bongo drum or a set of bells without ever writing notation or reading it. They can also perform and respond to music without involving any reading process at all.

For English literacy, would we be satisfied if children just *created* stories, *performed* stories, and *responded* to stories rather than learning to read them and write them down?

When asked if "Creating, Performing, and Responding" is what we want from music education, I say it isn't enough. We want children to learn the basics of reading standard music notation and be able to read it fluently.

Someday I hope to see music standards written as:

- Reading and writing standard music notation
- Creating
- Performing
- Responding

Until we clearly state that reading notation is a goal we should accomplish in early grades, I'm concerned that the majority of children across the nation won't receive the necessary training to read and write music literature. In other words, children in school won't be musically literate—no matter how much creating, performing, and responding they engage in.

Addendum 3

Aural Myths in General Music

Sometimes when you try to make changes in the school curriculum, such as instituting a new program for reading music, you will encounter a lot of push back from individuals who are adamantly against early notational reading programs. Invariably, teachers who don't believe in early instruction in music notation will present you with very important sounding philosophies of teaching that will mow you down if you are not prepared ahead of time with facts and ideas to support your point of view.

In this section, I will discuss a few ideas that dominate the aural-based curriculum in general music so that everyone can recognize how notational reading is being overlooked in our schools.

Aural Myth Number 1: *Children should only learn to read notation when they show that they are ready.*

The Rebuttal: We don't wait for children in school to be ready to learn the English language or to learn math. We start reading-readiness in PreK and continue increasing skills over time as a well-planned year-by-year program. In a similar manner, children will greatly benefit from age-appropriate early notational reading programs because these programs will also support the development of the long neural pathways for reading that lead to higher order thinking.

Furthermore, those who advocate for the concept of 'readiness' in music intelligence abilities assume that more aural training will help a child avoid reading notation awkwardly when they join a band or orchestra program. However, when you know the science of shorter and longer neurons, you can understand that the shorter aural-type neurons located near the ears have no relationship to the growth and development of the long neurons for reading that begin at the eyes.

Aural Myth Number 2: *Children will become ready to read music notation only after they complete an extensive program of performing and responding to rhythms first.*

The Rebuttal: The premise behind the "rhythm-first" philosophy is for students to learn music concepts in the order that those concepts appeared on the earth. This premise supposes that the first organized sounds came from cave men beating tree stumps for the fun of it and then later evolved into experimenting with sounds on animal horns and the strings of an archery bow.

The hierarchy just described is not the evolution of *music*. It's the evolution of *musical instruments*. Drums, then horns, then strings.

But I submit that the origins of *music* came long before boys and men discovered tree trunks. One of the most primal activities on earth is the act of giving birth. Newborns cry a lot. Mothers instinctively want to calm them and quiet them. Therefore, I believe the first repeated patterns were from mothers instinctively vocalizing soft sounds to coo their babies to sleep. As the first babies developed more awareness, mothers may have amused their babies by coaxing them to imitate the mother's vocal sounds that eventually became language. When parents and children walked in the woods, they may have imitated bird songs and other sounds from nature. Parents may also have clicked their tongues in a rhythmic pattern to get their children's attentions or vocalized in a rhythmic pattern.

In summary, music is as old as life itself. There is no way to surmise which appeared first—rhythm or pitch.

Instead of relying on a fixed philosophy like "rhythm first" or "pitch first" as we design the music curriculum of modern times, we need to ask ourselves what children need. If children are capable of learning pitches on student xylophones in kindergarten, why should they be limited only to tapping on tambourines, triangles, and wood blocks? While preschool children are learning to recognize geometric and letter shapes in preparation for reading words, they are equally capable of recognizing simple forms of music notation. For example, young students can easily draw or read a simple vertical line representing the stem of a quarter note, without the black notehead (meaning "clap") and a vertical squiggle line representing a quarter rest (meaning "don't clap"). Cardboard cards can be held up for everyone in class to see. The cards might show four beat patterns such as *line, line, line, squiggle*. The students would perform the pattern as clap, clap, clap, and then wave their hands apart, meaning "don't clap." Or for the rest, they might place their finger vertically on their lips while making a "Shh" sound for the quarter rest.

In the same manner, during PreK lessons, students can begin learning the CAT and DOG story for Companion Words to develop the visual skills for staff reading. (See Addendum 5 for a prepared CAT and DOG script for the teacher.)

Aural Myth Number 3: *Children should experiment with iconic notation before beginning formal training in music notation.*

The Rebuttal: Iconic notation is a primitive, creative system of writing down musical sounds sometimes using dots or lines or circles. There is nothing wrong with trying to introduce this in early grades if the children seem ready for it. This type of exercise is very useful for experiencing the logic of symbolism—learning that *written symbols represent ideas.*

However, we rob children of the ability to fully develop their brains when we only teach experimentation through iconic notation and refuse to give them an early start reading the notation that is standard in our society.

Imagine if we taught English literacy by taking a year or two for children to first make up their own alphabet? And yet, that's exactly how we've been treating music literacy in lower grades developing iconic notation instead of standard notation.

Addendum 4

The Loop System of Counting

As you read the basic principles of this method, I strongly suggest you actually try out the motions I describe. By physically experiencing the suggested motions, you will be aware of the potential benefits of this method.

The Loop Counting Method provides the necessary spatial intelligence experience the student needs to understand the downbeat and upbeat that are so necessary for musical expression while reading notation. Other methods that vocalize rhythmic symbols are linear and do not help the student experience the weight of the downbeat or the lifting feeling of the upbeat. Not only that, but vocalized rhythm methods are hardly practical for a woodwind or brass player who is blowing into their instrument. Even if they tried to hear the vocalized syllables in their head as they played, the imagined sound of the vocalized syllables would greatly interfere with the student's ability to hear what the horn is producing. It's much better for the musician to experience the down and upbeats of the written music through toe-tapping or even nodding the head while reading and playing the music.

Loop Counting can be experienced in four different ways:

- First, as a clapping method for the musician to act out the rhythmic symbols on the page. For example, a written quarter note would be clapped by bringing the hands together and keeping them together as the hands are brought downward, then upward (indicating that the sound of the quarter note is comprised of a downbeat and upbeat). When the hands return to the starting position, they separate, indicating that the quarter note is finished. A quarter rest would take the same amount of time with the hands going down and up, but the hands would not touch, indicating that there is no sound.

- Second, as a graphic method. The musician can draw loop pencil marks beneath notation on the page. (Drawing a "U" mark with a solid black line indicates one beat of sound that indicates the down and up motion of the downbeat and upbeat. A loop or "U" shape drawn with a dotted or broken line, indicates silence during the down and up direction of the beat.)

- Third, as a mental exercise. Rather than clapping or writing the loops, the musician can envision loops mentally. This means, the musician would look at the written symbols and *think* the corresponding down-up loops.

- Fourth, for composing music. It's easy to think of the sounds first, then write the length of the sounds on paper by using a pencil to draw the down-up loops while humming the tune. As a final step, the musician would translate the simple loop-type notation into standard notation such as quarter notes and rests.

By following the Loop Counting Method, students can go all the way from Level One rhythms (greater than one beat) to advanced counting skills using sixteenth notes, ties, and 6/8 time. Because this method starts with simple forms of rhythm and proceeds to advanced forms of rhythms, we say it is based on logical hierarchy. This means the knowledge is very stable and will not fade easily. Students gain confidence in their abilities because they are able to reach advanced levels very quickly and easily.

Clapping the Loops

Level One Rhythms: Here's how to clap rhythms that are one beat and greater:

- For a quarter note, clasp your hands and move them down, then up in a single down-and-up motion. Separate the hands when they return to starting position. Each time the hands move downward, say the number of the count. Each time the hands move upward, say "and."

- For a half note, move your clasped hands down-up-down-up, in one continuous motion before separating them, representing two beats. (Example of counting: "One-and-two-and.")

- For a whole note, clasp your hands and move them down-and-up four times for four beats. Do not unclasp your hands until the note is complete. (Example of counting: "One-and-two-and-three-and-four-and.")

- For rests, follow the same instructions to move down-and-up, but this time, while moving downward, hold your hands apart but parallel, palms facing each other (rather than clasped). When you draw rests on paper, use broken lines rather than solid lines.

Level Two Rhythms: This is where the Loop Clapping System really empowers the student to visualize the divisions of the beat using spatial intelligence. Unlike vocal syllables for reading rhythms that are linear in design, loop-counting demonstrates spatial intelligence characteristics for duration—the *distance* the hands travel, going down and up on every beat.

Here's how to clap Level Two divisions of the beat:

- For the first eighth note that begins the duplet, clasp the hands and move them downward, then release them (because that eighth note is finished. For the second eighth note in the duplet, clasp the hands where the last eighth note ended (at the bottom of the loop) and bring the clasped hands upward. When the hands are up all the way, unclasp them because the upbeat is finished. On downbeats say the number of the count, and on upbeats say the word "and."

- For triplets (three eighth notes per beat), think of one long "U" shape divided into three equal segments (rather than focusing on a down and up beat). Just remember to clasp and unclasp your hands to indicate three separate sounds moving along the loop path. The wrong approach is allowing the hands to "pop" together and immediately fly apart, the way people normally clap. Instead, your hands stay clasped along the loop line for each individual note to show length and duration.

- Sixteenths (four sixteenths per beat) are easy—clap two segments on the way down in the loop (two sixteenths during the downbeat) and two segments on the way up (during the upbeat). (Two sixteenths on the downbeat and two sixteenths on the upbeat.) The words on the way down are "One-eee." The words on the way up are "And-uh."

- Combinations of eighths and sixteenths:
  - For one eighth followed by two sixteenths, clasp your hands all the way down during the downbeat, saying "One-eee." Then start at the bottom of the loop, clasp hands for the first half of the way up (saying 'and'), take hands apart halfway up, and reconnect the hands for the remaining distance going up (saying "uh"). Take hands apart at the top.
  - For two sixteenths followed by one eighth, reverse the process by showing two segments on the way down and one long segment on the way up. (On the way down say "One-eee." On the way up, "and-uh.")

Drawing the Loops

Loop clapping and counting easily translates to pencil marks. (Just as a reminder, this activity corresponds to **Spatial Intelligence Principle #4**: The ability to produce a *"graphic likeness of spatial information."*)

The student can draw pencil marks on blank paper to represent notation while taking music dictation. Or pencil marks can be written under the notation in the student's lesson book.

In the Loop Counting Method, the student can:

- Draw the loops for quarter notes as a solid U-shaped line.
- Draw duplets as a broken loop (\ /) that is split open at the bottom, (where the hands would separate when clapping them).
- Draw rests as dotted lines instead of solid black lines.
- Draw quadruplets (four sixteenth notes) as a "V" shape where each of the downward and upward lines are written as two segments moving downward or upward instead of one long line.

Advantages of Loops

There are seven significant advantages to using the Loop Counting Method:

1. In the general music classroom, children can take turns "playing teacher" by clapping loops for their classmate, who either draws the sounds as loops (V or \ /) or claps the example back to the "teacher." Also, the child playing "teacher" can demonstrate a quarter followed by two eighth notes on a student xylophone and the "student" can either clap the sound in loops or write the loops down. If the loops are written down, the "student" can also write alphabet letters under the loops to indicate the pitches that were used in the example. (This is a visual exercise. The "student" watches the "teacher" strike the xylophone and therefore knows

the name of the pitches, which are usually written on the xylophone bars.)

2. Understanding the quarter note as a down and up motion (downbeat and upbeat) prepares the student to later learn the down and up motions in duplet divisions of the beat.

3. The loop method makes it possible to visualize that *rests* require the same duration as notes. (A quarter note is written as a solid U-shaped line. A quarter rest is written as a dotted or broken U-shape line.)

4. The dotted quarter (for one-and-a-half beats) is very easy to visualize through the demonstrated loop method. (It requires three half beats such as down-up-down.) Likewise, ties are easily visualized when the student understands where all the half beats (downbeats and upbeats) are located within the tie.

5. When students learn to draw the loops in perfect alignment beneath the music notation on the staff, they are *reinforcing the same spatial/kinesthetic skills* they will use in the general classroom for aligning numbers in multiplication and division.

6. Best of all, for the teacher, the Loop Counting System solves the problem of deciphering what is taking place in the student's mind as he or she counts the music. In a private lesson, the teacher will notice any confusion or lack of knowledge immediately when the student writes the loops under a difficult counting passage. In a classroom with many students, the teacher can glance around the entire classroom and notice which students are clapping the loops and processing the rhythms correctly.

7. Writing loops beneath a passage of music makes a good homework assignment or silent work while other students in the classroom are being tested.

Addendum 5

Classroom Management for Student Xylophone Lessons

Two of my goals, as I taught lessons for student xylophones in kindergarten through 3rd grade in general music, were for students to first learn eye-hand coordination needed for instrumental music (as well as reading in the general classroom). And second, to interpret symbolism (just reading alphabet letters, at first, and later reading standard notation).

To accomplish these two goals in reading notation, I set up my classroom much differently than I would have for exploration and creativity centers.

For instance, the xylophones were arranged ahead of time in straight rows on the floor, facing the front of the room where the music notation or pitch letter names would be shown on a screen or smartboard. Sometimes I had a fully carpeted music room where children were comfortable sitting on the floor; other times I had a pile of rectangular rug remnants. Each child would bring their "mat" and place it in front of their xylophone to sit.

My aim was to make instrumental technique regimented and correct but fun. When I say regimented, I'm talking about *establishing* routines and guidelines that students could anticipate and rely on. This cut down on the number of random distractions in the classroom involving the instruments and mallets so students could focus on the lesson and really enjoy learning.

I am fully aware that many of us have been conditioned to reject all forms of regimentation in an elementary classroom. From the 1960s on, direct teaching was frowned upon while experimentation was recommended. But now we have neurological proof through electronic imaging that reading takes place on the long neurons that must be directly trained. Part of that direct training includes setting up routines that will foster good habits and cut down on children straying off topic or engaging in distracting behavior that interrupts learning. A teacher is not being mean by insisting on behaviors that support learning. Just the opposite—children find comfort in routine and established expectations. Furthermore, they welcome rules when they see how much they are able to accomplish during lessons.

I asked my students to "walk—don't run" to a xylophone and sit cross-legged, facing the screen. If they ran, I asked them to get up, return to the doorway, and show me again how they should go to their instrument. This type of correction would set the tone for other children to listen carefully and follow the given directions. By adhering to these routine rules, children avoided falling on the sharp metal edges of the xylophone bars and injuring themselves.

When each of my PreK through second grade children first sat next to their xylophone, they were not given a mallet. I asked that they put their hands on their knees (to stop them from banging on the bars with their fingers). Only then did I bring out the mallets, held in my hand like a bouquet of flowers.

"These are my flowers," I would say, "but they are really mallets. Can you all say 'mallets?'" After their response, I would continue, "As I give you one of these, hold it up like a flower and tell me what color your flower is." The idea of choosing a color for their flower immediately delighted children because they felt heard and acknowledged for their answer. The flower idea gave me the excuse for everyone to hold up their mallet in a ready position, rather than going wild hitting the xylophones. Yes, at first, I did have to keep reminding them to hold up their "flower," but my gentle reminders paid off in the long run.

Next, I trained the children using the directives "playing position" and "play." I showed them that 'playing position' meant holding the "flower" (head of the mallet) about 3 inches above the key we wanted to strike. I would wait until all the mallets were in position. Sometimes, as twenty-eight mallets from twenty-eight children froze with anticipation, it was so quiet in the room that the air felt electric.

Then I'd say, "Play," and twenty-eight mallets would strike the bar. Invariably, those who missed the xylophone bar would try again and taps would continue for a few seconds. But eventually, students' eye-hand coordination improved. Eventually, all of the students learned to strike together. This little game was repeated every time we used the xylophones. To make it more interesting each time, I would change the pitches. And eventually we would "play" every tone in the C scale.

Each class time, after we reoriented to the directives "playing position" and "play," we would play short exercises and songs from the screen. Sometimes I would give them "free practice" where every child would read and play the exercises on their own. If the room became too chaotic, I might ask them to practice the song by using just their finger to strike the bars or use the stick end of the mallet. When it came time to stop the free practice, all I would have to do is raise my own mallet into a vertical position and say "Flower." All the children's mallets would come up into the air.

Contrary to what many educators believe, children are relaxed and ready to learn in this kind of organized environment. Once they learn what is expected of them, they know what's coming and they begin concentrating on the lesson. Also, a lesson filled with objectives the children are already familiar with lessens the need for the teacher to raise his or her voice or to scold students for misbehavior. An organized room contributes to happier children and joyful learning.

I remember when the methods for direct teaching were almost totally dropped in the 1970s in favor of exploration and self-discovery, but we should remember that Swiss psychologist Jean Piaget (1896-1980) approved of direct teaching methods. While there is certainly a need for exploration in learning aural skills, a class of twenty-eight students will only learn proper instrumental technique and visual skills for spatial intelligence and reading in a structured environment. Without consistent order in the classroom, music class with student xylophones can turn into a disaster. Instruments can be damaged, injuries can occur, and children can leave the classroom dissatisfied.

Children don't enjoy experiencing chaos at school. So don't be afraid to plan ahead how to instruct children on where to sit, how they will treat the equipment, and even how they will exit the room.

Another important factor to remember when deciding how strict the classroom rules will be is that our goal should be to train students to monitor their own behavior. By always waiting to strike the xylophone, observing playing position, and learning to put equipment away, children learn to eventually do these things without being told. They learn to be responsible and respectful—of others and of the equipment. When this kind of training begins in kindergarten, it will benefit students for years to come as they move on to play recorders and keyboards.

Addendum 6

Introducing Companion Words in Early Childhood

Preparation: Before children use the Companion Words script, the teacher should introduce the children to the patterns of black keys on the piano keyboard and teach them how they can identify the white key C.

HAND GESTURES: During the script, the teacher should gesture toward the poster (with the non-dominant hand) at the same time an adult term is spoken. The teacher should gesture toward the children (with the dominant hand) at the same time the children's term (CAT or DOG is spoken.

This system of hand gestures trains children to immediately see that the story is being transformed into their make-believe world. They will feel the story is very important when they "see" that it is connected to adult information. What's more, the dual hand-gestures show them they can use the adult term interchangeably with their term, whenever they wish.

Poster-by-Poster Script for Introducing Companion Words

(***Instructor, pointing to Poster 1***) *Today we are going to have a story called "Music Cat."*

*What you see is really a music staff, but we are going to call it a **building**. This big swirly sign here is a Treble-clef sign telling you we are in the Land of the **Right Hand**. Everyone, raise your right hand.*

*(**For Poster 2**) Notice the music note sitting under the building. We are going to call it CAT. Notice the line going through its face. In music we call that line a ledger line, but today we are calling it the cat's **whisker**. You will always know it's CAT if you look for the whisker.*

What letter does CAT start with?(Wait for response.)

Can we each go to the piano keyboard and take turns showing where the cat lives on the keys? Try to use your right hand.

(For Poster 3) *In our story, CAT has a friend—DOG—who also lives under the building. You will know it's DOG when you notice that it doesn't have a whisker.*

You'll also know CAT and DOG because they always live under the building. CAT and DOG are good friends. They are not allowed to go inside. Maybe they've dug a hole for themselves under the building to keep warm.

Let's go find DOG on the white keys. He lives on the right side of CAT. Press the DOG on the keyboard. Then press the CAT again, too.

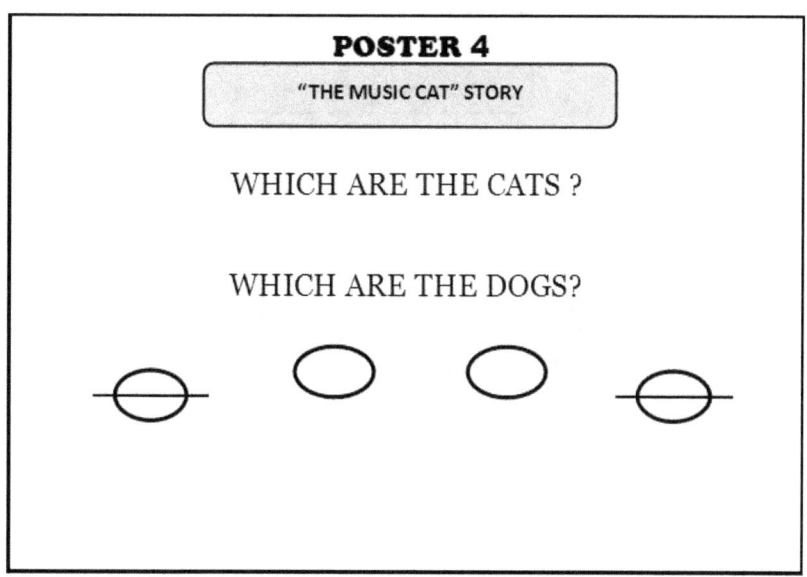

(For Poster 4) *Where do you see CATs and DOGs in the poster? Remember that CATs have whiskers—DOGs do not.*

First tell me what you see (read the whole line).

Now go to the keyboard and play each of the CATs and DOGs. Remember to play them from left to right.

Next, we will take paper and pencils to draw our own CATs and DOGs.

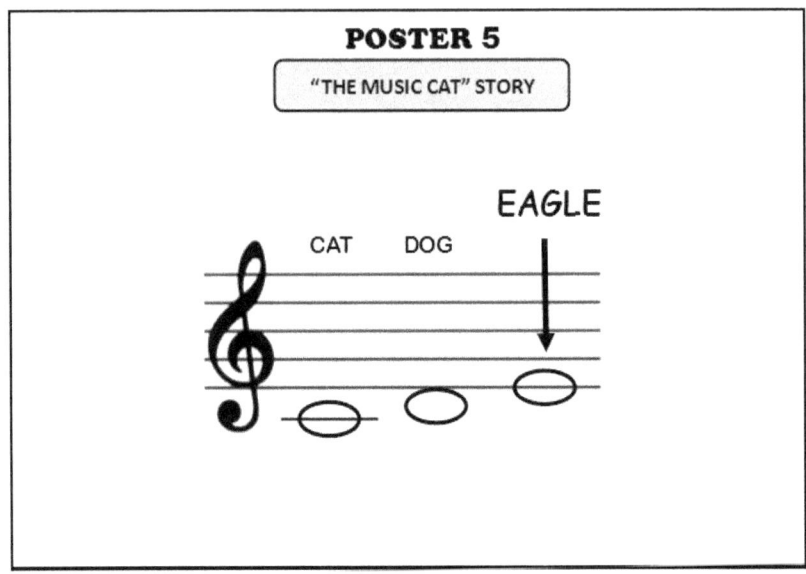

(For Poster 5) One day, CAT and DOG looked up and saw a large bird circling overhead. It came closer and closer, and soon it swooped down onto the first step of the house.

"My name is EAGLE," said the bird. "Would it be okay with you if I built my nest right here on the first step of your house?" At first, CAT and DOG felt a little jealous because they weren't allowed to ever sit on the first step of the house! But they liked how majestic EAGLE looked. They liked watching him fly around and then land on the first step, so gracefully. So, EAGLE stayed.

Can you find CAT, DOG, then EAGLE (the E key) on your piano and press each of them three times?

Note To Teacher: It's important to emphasize that the first step or line is always at the bottom of the staff, not at the top. We count upward in music, not downward. That's why we say the eagle landed on the "first" step.

Once students can read C, D, and E from the staff, they can be introduced to short songs like Hot Cross Buns and Mary Had a Little Lamb in order to practice reading from the Treble Staff. They can sing these short songs from the music staff by using the words "E-D-C." They can use Kodaly hand signals as they sing E, D, and C from the staff. I highly recommend that any written notation at this stage of note reading does not contain words for lyrics or any pictures.

To further solidify spatial recognition of these three pitches on the staff, I also recommend students take ownership of these pitches by creating their own 4-beat measures, drawing the pitches as whole notes at the bottom of a (pre-drawn) treble staff. The teacher can then put these creations on a bulletin board for children to try out. Or the teacher can draw them larger on charts everyone in the room can read together. Or put them on an overhead projector that everyone can sing from at once. Be sure to include each composer's name so they can take pride in their composition. After children can sing these compositions, they can be used for learning centers in the room as children rotate freely to try the examples on xylophones of various sizes, electronic keyboards, glass water bottles (be mindful of safety), or other pitched instruments.

When the teacher is ready to introduce the F and G on the lower treble clef, the teacher can amplify the story to include FOX and GORILLA or GOAT.

Continue to Poster 6 when you are ready to introduce the students to reading pitches with the left hand on the Bass Clef, such as in beginning keyboard classes or private lessons. This might be reserved for fourth grade if children have access to electronic keyboards where they will learn to read and play bass and treble tones at the same time.

(For Poster 6 for keyboards in late 3rd or 4th Grade or earlier in private music lessons) One day, CAT wandered down the big hill from Treble Land to Bass Land to visit his friend, BEAR, who was sitting on the roof of her underground home.

From now on you will have to look carefully every time you see CAT to notice if he is home by his building or if he is down where BEAR lives.

(For Poster 7) *Let's go to Bass Land to practice reading and playing the CATs and BEARs. Hold up your left thumb. Say "CAT!" (Wait for student response.) Hold up your left pointer finger. Say "BEAR!"(Wait for student response.) Let's go to the keyboard and put our left thumb on the C key. Let's play exercise number one. Remember that CATs have the whisker lines. (Then play exercise number two.)*

(For Poster 8) "What's that funny sound?" said CAT one day.

"Oh," said BEAR, "those are the ANTs marching on the top of my house!"

Sure enough, there they were—a gazillion ANTs marching on the top line of the building, singing, "The Ants Go Marching One by One, Hurrah, Hurrah. . . . " *(Allow students to sing some of this song if they know it.)*

Let's go find BEARs and ANTs on the keyboard. *(Class moves to keyboard in the classroom to take turns finding the appropriate white keys.)*

Introducing Companion Words in Early Childhood

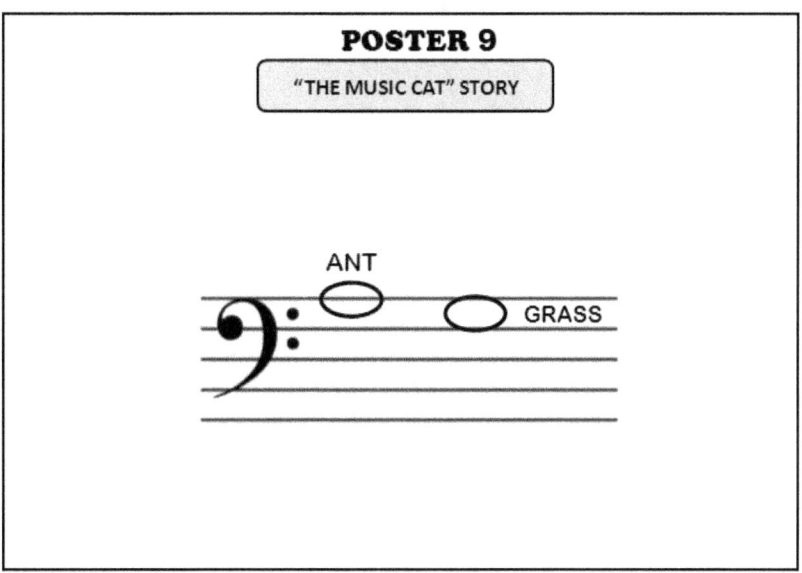

(FOR POSTER 9) *The clamoring of the ANTs along the roof line was noisy and growing louder. CAT put his paws over his ears and made a face. "What are we going to do about this, BEAR?" he shrieked.*

BEAR just shrugged her shoulders and sluffed back into a round ball on the roof.

"Okay, if you won't do anything, I will!" remarked CAT, who reached down with his paw and shook the A Line hard as he could.

ANTs flew this way and that. Then he shook it even harder. Most of them tumbled onto the music space directly below.

"Very clever," laughed BEAR. "You knocked the ANTs into the GRASS!"

"That's right," said CAT. "But at least we'll have a little peace tonight. The ANTs-are-in-the-GRASS."

"The ANTs-are-in-the-GRASS," repeated BEAR.

"I'm not in the GRASS!" said the biggest ANT, in a huff, still marching on her line. "You didn't knock **me** off. Visit away, if you must, but I'm never giving up my A-line."

BEAR and CAT smiled. They had what they wanted—enough peace and quiet to sing all night.

Let's find ANT on the keyboard and make it go into the GRASS. (Play A, then G).

(For Poster 10): What do you see in the poster? Are there any CATs? Any DOGs? First say what you see. Then play what you see.

> **NOTE to TEACHER**: This story does a good job of introducing these pitches on the bass clef, but the story alone may not be enough to teach the positions of these pitches on the keyboard. However, there are supplemental ways the teacher can reinforce some of the basic concepts.
>
> Get creative! For instance, you can stretch out a jump rope in the classroom and use paper clips to attach index cards (even colored index cards) containing large black "A" letters to the rope so the letters are "on the line." Students can have fun knocking some of the ANTs off the line into the "GRASS," which could be a green blanket or piece of cloth on the floor. Then by returning to the staff, children will be better able to associate "ANT" and "GRASS" as belonging next to each other on the staff and on the piano keys.
>
> In a private music lesson, a teacher wouldn't have to go to all this effort. But we all know that in a class of twenty-eight or more students, many students are mentally on the outskirts of our lessons unless we find dynamic ways to entice them in.
>
> Later, when students use electronic keyboards and can't remember what key is to the right of G, or to the left of A on the white keys, all the teacher has to do is say, in a sing-song manner, "The ANT is in the GRASS. The ANT is in the GRASS."

The End

Small Nuances that Improve Companion Words

Here are some guidelines that are helpful when using the Companion Words script:

For one, children don't want to be lied to. The teacher should never point to a whole note and say, "This is a cat." Perhaps eighty percent of students may be willing to accept whatever the teacher says—even if the teacher says the sky is purple—but others will distrust a teacher who doesn't speak the truth. And that small minority of children are correct—a whole note is not a cat.

In effect, it's better to indicate through words and actions that the adult term exists but, instead, "we" are going to play a game and call it whatever "we" like. That kind of explanation remains true to the underlying premise of make-believe—that we can turn the *real world* into the child's *imaginative world*. So, it's better to point to the whole note and say, "This is a music note, but we are going to *call* it a cat."

Children really appreciate the teacher who will bring information into their style of learning, instead of dragging them into the confusing web of adult words and concepts. And just as a reminder, *imagination* is very important in learning about notation because it helps students process adult abstractions. We learned this from the 2015 Amherst study, which showed that imagination is located in the same region of the brain as abstractions, naming, and symbolism.

I'm not being overly picky when I say that the teacher's hand gestures are central to the constant shift between adult and imaginary concepts. When the new companion word is being introduced, if the teacher *consistently* uses one hand to emphasize the adult term and the opposite hand for the Companion Word, children "see" the consistent *transfer* of information from the real world into their imaginative world. This visual memory of watching information transfer from one of the teacher's hands to the other teaches the student that there are two versions of the concept. This will greatly facilitate the child's ability to relinquish the imaginative name later in favor of the adult's formal name for the symbol.

I usually present Companion Words while I stand next to my slide screen or smart board at my left, so that I use my weaker left hand for the adult information on the staff and my dominant right hand for gesturing toward the children to emphasize their imaginary names and terms.

Consistently remembering to make a habit of saying the adult term first, then the imaginary term, helps me to never omit the adult abstract name (such as "whole note") that I eventually want each of the students to hear, remember, and understand.

Think of the advantages of using a story like this instead of the old way of lecturing and having children memorize rules. From the first sentence of the Companion Word story, the children are completely engaged. They are playing the appropriate keys on the piano by reading real music symbols from the music staff.

In addition, children learn that notes on the page are connected to their instrument. They learn that the horizontal ledger line is an important characteristic for identifying Middle C. And they learn that the presence or absence of the ledger line gives them the ability to differentiate C from other pitches on the page.

The Concept of "Location" in Early Lessons

Slides 2, 3, and 4 teach the C and D whole notes *with* the staff. Here great emphasis must be placed on the concept of *below*. The children need to know that CAT and DOG live *under the building (under* the staff*)*. It's important to emphasize *location* (spatial recognition) through creative storytelling to embellish the concept of *beneath*.

"Under the staff" is very abstract. But it can be taught through the feelings of an imaginary cat and dog who, for instance, are sad because they are always told to live outside—in the rain, in the snow. They must stay beneath the staff "building." Because they can never go into the building, they become grouchy when Eagle flies down and sits on the first step (the first line of the staff). Imagination is very effective for engaging the child's emotions to reinforce music concepts. And again, the 2015 Amherst Study verifies that imagination is located in the same part of the brain as symbolism, naming, and abstractions.

Another concept that is easy to teach through imagination in early childhood is *duration*. The cat (whole note), which is first associated with a four-beat sound, can be altered in shape to look like a half note by saying it's a **"white cat with a pole."**

The child can physically act out the half note by pretending to *be* CAT, by holding a pencil vertically and pressing their foot to the floor while chanting "One, two."

By altering the half note and shading in the circle part, the half note becomes a quarter note, a "**black cat with a pole**." Black cats can march *on* the beat! Thus, through play and imagination, children become familiar with the idea that different shapes represent timing.

Rests are just as easy to learn. By introducing a squiggle line called "Shh" (instead of the abstract name "rest," or "quarter rest"), the rhythmic variations for C and D, using quarter notes and rests become plentiful. For example: *C, C, Shh, C.* Or the variation: *C, Shh, C, Shh.*

The main idea in teaching instrumental music is to provide enough rhythmic variations so each level of pitch proficiency can be mastered and established before proceeding to higher levels with new pitches. In general music classes, once the children can read the C, D, and E pitches, the remaining general music classes that year can reinforce these pitches through learning centers, through groups of two playing "teacher" and "student" and by lots of reading of these pitches in variations of quarter notes, quarter rests, half notes, and whole notes. That way, as the students move on to the next grade in elementary school, they will be able to add one or two more pitches to the pitches they already know. We don't have to be in a hurry to teach new concepts. Rather, it works better to reinforce the basics. The aim is not to produce total musicianship in early grades but to present students with a working knowledge of how notes are read from the staff. In doing so, even with simple examples such as C, D, and E, we train students' visual skills and music intelligence capabilities. And most of all, we establish a solid foundation upon which to build true music literacy for every student, not just those who will join band or orchestra.

Addendum 7

Classroom Example of Lap-to-Instrument Technique

My flute students had great success with this technique in eliminating their confusion between the fingering for "D" (covering six finger holes with *no pinky finger*) and the similar fingering for "E" (five finger holes *plus the pinky finger*). Their confusion always occurred when toggling back and forth between two considerations—whether to use the pinky or not and whether to cover the right fourth finger hole. Much time can be wasted in a music lesson with fingering errors like this, so my students needed a method that would remediate problems quickly.

The way we corrected their pinky problem was by using the Lap-to-Instrument Technique that I developed. It started with them setting the flute on a table and picking it up again, going directly to the D fingering. After they mastered the D fingering without wobbly fingers or any hesitation, they practiced picking up their flute and going directly to their finger pattern for E.

The next step was to drill back and forth on these two finger patterns. I would call out "E" or "D" at random as they reached for the flute on the table. They would have to quickly determine which fingering would be used. With patience and practice, they were eventually able to consistently send their fingers accurately to the D and E fingerings.

The reason this drill was effective was because it only involved their fingers, not their mouth or lips or wind.

We were getting closer to mastering D and E in their music—but we weren't there yet. They still needed to practice D and E, back and forth, in succession. This meant overcoming another physical roadblock that most flute students encounter—the stiff and awkward feeling of lifting the right-hand ring finger off of the hole while the pinky is moving downward to press on its key.

After they learned to toggle back and forth between D and E, I presented them with musical passages containing successive Ds and Es. This meant they would demonstrate their new technical skills while producing the tone and keeping a steady beat.

Addendum 8

The Backwards Method

The following descriptions explain how to instruct a student who seems unable to understand how the lines and spaces of the staff work even after months of music training. The Backwards Method teaches the student to take tones from the instrument and write them on the staff instead of the way students normally start out by reading notational information from the staff and transferring it to the instrument.

Sometimes, part of the problem is that lesson books usually introduce students to the treble staff beginning with Middle C and D below the staff. This alone is a learning trap because it's difficult to envision how the ledger line for Middle C is actually part of an imaginary staff line, labeled C.

In addition to that type of confusion, even the first three letters of the C scale sound like an unfamiliar grouping: C-D-E. If instead, the teacher will begin students higher on the staff, beginning on the A space (in the key of a-minor), right away there will be a familiarity with the grouping of letters A-B-C for beginning reading exercises.

Another gimmick that will help the confused student is preparing special staff paper for them. The teacher can print staff paper with three or four sets of staves that each begin with the G-clef sign at the left. Then, for each staff, the teacher places a row of large light-gray letters on the second space spelling AAAAA . . . from left to right across the entire staff. The letters can be placed on the space using a graphics computer program or handwritten with a highlighter pen before making multiple copies printed in black and white.

Then, using the pre-printed staff paper, the teacher asks the student to draw a bar line at the end of each staff line with a third bar line directly in the middle, creating two measures per line. The student should be advised to always first divide the staves into measures in the coming weeks before using the staves to compose their own music.

Next, the teacher places capital letters above the first measure with the instructions, "These are the pitches we are using for this measure. Listen as I sing them and write the pitches on the staff lines."

The teacher might write A B above the first measure and then sing, "A, A, B, B." The student must then write two quarter notes on the A space and two on the B line. This shouldn't be difficult because the A space is already labeled by large gray A letters from left to right. If the student is able to write these first two pitches correctly, the student demonstrates to themselves that they understand that music proceeds left to right and that they've figured out where B is located. Be sure to remind them that the alphabet moves upward on the staff.

When I did this with my nine-year-old student, she tried to draw the B quarter note on the third space (the C space) This told me right away that she didn't understand that the staff uses lines and spaces in succession. Of course, I had already told her this many times before. But on this occasion, she had to physically erase the incorrect answer and replace it with the correct answer. I think the act of her having to physically erase the incorrect answer made more of a kinesthetic impression than just listening aurally to my directions. She did not make that mistake again in successive examples. Perhaps this was an indication that she is a kinesthetic learner. Just hearing the information and seeing the information was not enough. She needed to use the physical lines and spaces to understand the underlying principles that govern them.

> The more I understand how children learn, the more convinced I am that reading music, in some form or other, is possible for every average and above average individual. If children can't read notes, it's not the children who have failed; instead, we—the educators—have failed to adequately present the material in a form they can use. We must keep ardently improving our delivery methods, our testing, and our remediation.

Getting back to my story of the student and the Backwards Method, as the student and I proceeded measure by measure, I increased the difficulty of the examples of dictation in the following manner: (A B A B) (A B B A) (A B C C) (C A B B) (A C C C) (C A C A). On the last examples, I only demonstrated the pitches by singing "Ah", not singing the names of the letters. She wrote these "Ah" tones correctly on the staff, indicating that she could not only hear steps and thirds, but that she could write these interval changes correctly on the staff. That surprised me. She wasn't below average in intelligence or in aural processing. She just had weak spatial intelligence skills for visually processing the lines and spaces of the music staff.

Then we went to the piano. I played four-beat examples of A-B-C on the piano keys while she wrote the examples on the staff. I also asked her to play some of the examples she had written.

In the weeks that followed, we repeated the A-B-C letter exercise in other areas of the staff, using F-G-A and (third space) C-D-E. I encouraged her to write songs that took up the whole page using one of the three note samples. Each week, her confidence in reading from the staff greatly increased.

The conclusion we should draw from this example is that among a school class of twenty-eight children, there may be several students who are kinesthetic learners. They learn more by doing than listening. That's why it's a good idea to always include a lot of pitch and rhythm *dictation* in any notational reading program. At first, rhythm dictation works well on plain unruled paper. But eventually, students need to place pitch information on the music staff. Then ultimately, rhythm information should be added to the pitches so they no longer just write pitches as all quarter notes but also as half notes, whole notes, and eighth notes.

Again, I truly believe that all average and above-average learners can gain a working knowledge of the music staff—providing we are creative enough to find the methods that work. Conversely, we greatly short-change the greater population of our students when we don't offer notational reading to everyone in school.

Addendum 9

Keeping the "Fun" in Learning Alphabetic Adjacency

Our challenge in our schools is to help children have fun while they are learning. Silly, giddy games and exercises can make the learning environment *appear* to be "fun." But it doesn't compare to the deeper fun that comes when children realize they are accomplishing something important, even if it requires a little work.

This next idea helps children not only develop good fixed-order skills but allows them to record their progress and show that progress to their parents.

As children approach third grade and beyond, they begin searching for relevance in school activities, especially in general music classes. If they feel that the subject they are studying is important, they are enthusiastic. If they feel lessons are just busy work, they tune out. Having them see progress on a chart, take the chart home, and then experience how their new skills emerge even farther can be a strong motivator for children to understand that music is not only fun but important.

To begin, the children in a general music classroom might be given a personal blank grid chart designed to keep track of how many alphabetic skills they have learned. To foster the "fun" idea, this chart could be pasted upon a clever cut out in the shape of a leaf, an ice cream cone, or some other kid friendly shape. Over a period of a few weeks, as each student demonstrates they can recite A to G (a step-wise skill), a sticker would be placed on their chart. Saying the letters backwards from G to A would earn them another sticker. The chart could also record their ability to recite letters that show how to skip letters, complete three-letter clusters, and identify neighboring letters.

When the chart is complete, the child could experience closure through a two-minute process that would feel like a mini-ceremony or celebration—by having the child sign their name on the bottom, add the date of completion, and then watch the teacher sign the chart. This completed chart acts as tangible proof of accomplishment in music class that the student could take home to show parents. Of course, the wise teacher would help *everyone* in class finish this task so that all students complete their chart, learn, and grow through positive reinforcement.

The children would then be in a position to demonstrate their new knowledge of alphabetic order while exploring classroom learning centers where they would circulate around the room, trying out familiar and unfamiliar keyboard type instruments. This would give them the opportunity to practice playing and hearing tones that move step-wise, skip, are clustered or are directly adjacent (neighboring tones).

With some classes, I was able to set up a plastic-covered area for pouring water into bottles to either tap them or blow on the openings. Although somewhat messy and wet, this learning center was popular for children to create and explore intervals. The determining factor in the decision to include the water learning center was always how well the students in a particular class could work independently with moderate supervision.

Learning is rich and meaningful to students when they understand that their abilities are evolving.

Select Bibliography

Books

The American Heritage Dictionary of the English Language, Second College Edition. Houghton Mifflin Company. Boston, 1985.

Critical Issues in Music Education: Contemporary Theory and Practice. Abeles, Harold F. and Custodero, Lori A., editors. Oxford University Press, 2010.

The Development and Practical Application of Music Learning Theory. Runfola, Maria and Taggart, Cynthia Crump. GIA Publications, Inc. Chicago, 2005.

Feierabend, John M. *Conversation Solfege Level 1: Teachers Manual.* First Steps in Music, Inc. P.O. Box 73, Simsbury, CT, 1995. (Currently published by GIA Publications, Inc., Chicago, IL, 2000.)

Gardner, Howard. *Frames of Mind, The Theory of Multiple Intelligences.* Basic Books, Harper Collins Publishers, New York, 1983.

Gordon, Edwin E. *Learning Sequences in Music.* GIA Publications, Inc. Chicago, IL, 2012.

Gordon, Edwin E. *Untying Gordian Knots.* Meredith Music, division of GIA Publications, Inc. Chicago, IL, 2011.

The Harvard Dictionary of Music, Fourth Edition. Randel, Don Michael, editor. The Belknap Press of Harvard University Press. Cambridge, Massachusetts, and London, England. 2003.

The International Encyclopedia of Music and Musicians, Ninth Edition. Thompson, Oscar, editor. Dodd, Mead & Company. New York, 1964.

Articles

Adalf, Elena W.; Vaden, Ryan J.; Niver, Anastasia J.; Manuel, Allison F.; Onyilo, Vincent C.; Araujo, Matheus T.; Dieni, Christina V.; Vo, Hai T.; King, Gwendalyn D.; Wadiche, Jacques I.; Overstreet-Wadiche, Linda. **"Adult-born neurons modify excitatory synaptic transmission to existing neurons."** *eLife*. 2017, Jan. 30; 6: e19886. DOI: 10.7554/eLife.19886. www.ncbi.nlm.nih.gov/pmc/articles/PMC5279947

Balsters, J. H. and Ramnani N. **"Symbolic Representations of Action in the Human Cerebellum."** *Neuroimage.* 2008, 43 (2): 388-398. DOI:10. 1016/j.neuroimage. 2008.07.010. www.pubmed.ncbi.nlm.nih.gov/18692577

Brown, Timothy T. and Jernigan, Terry L. **"Brain Development During the Preschool Years."** *Neuropsychology Review 22,* pp 313-333. 2012. www.link.springer.com/article/10.1007/s11065-012-9214-1

Butzlaff, Ron. **"Can Music Be Used to Teach Reading?"** *The Journal of Aesthetic Education*, Vol. 34 No. 3-4, Special Issue: The Arts and Academic Achievement: What the Evidence Shows. (Autumn-Winter, 2000) pp 167-178. University of Illinois Press.

www.doi.org/10.2307/3333642

Fair, Damien A.; Cohen, Alexander L.; Power, Johnathan D.; Dosenbach, Nico U.F.; Church, Jessica A.; Meizin, Francis M.; Schlaggar, Braley L.; Petersen, Stephen E. **"Functional Brain Networks Develop from a**

'Local to Distributed' Organization." (2009) *PLoS Comput Biol* 5(5): e1000381. www.doi.org/10.1371/journal.pcbi.1000381

Hopkins, J. Roy. **"The Enduring Influence of Jean Piaget."** *Observer Magazine,* Vol. 24, Issue 10, Dec. 1, 2011. www.psychologicalscience.org/observer/jean-piaget

Mathews, Jay. **"21 Years Later, 'Multiple Intelligences' Still Debated."** *Washington Post*, 2004, September 7, Section A, page 9.

McLeod, S. A. **"Bruner Learning Theory in Education"** *Simply Psychology.* (2019, July 11). www.simplypsychology.org/bruner.html

Musumeci, Orlando. **"The Cognitive Pedagogy of Aural Training."** Published online through the *European Society for the Cognitive Sciences of Music* [ESCOM], 2000. www.escom.org/proceedings/ICMPC2000/poster/Musumeci.htm

Taylor, P.; Hobbs, J.N.; Burroni, J.; Siegelmann, H.T. **"The Global Landscape of Cognition: Hierarchical aggregation as an organizational principal of human cortical networks and functions."** *Scientific Reports*, December 2015: 5:18112 Dol: 10.1038/ srep 18112. www.reasearchgate.net/publication/287204525

www.ncbi.nlm.hig.gov/pmc/articles/PMC3681187/

Uytun, Merve Cikili. **"Development Period of the Prefrontal Cortex."** Oct. 3, 2018. (Chapter One of the book *Prefrontal Cortex,* edited by Ana Starcevic for the Department of Child and Adolescent Psychiatry, Kayseri Training and Research Hospital, Kayseri, Turkey.)

https://www.doi.org/10.5772/intechopen.73226

Websites for National Standards in Education

For Common Core State Standards Initiative:

www.corestandards.org/read-the-standards/

For Common Core English Language Arts Standards:

www.corestandards.org/ELA-Literacy/

For Common Core English Language Arts Standards » Reading: Foundational Skills » Kindergarten:

www.corestandards.org/ELA-Literacy/RF/K/

For National Core Arts Standards in Dance, Media Arts, Music, Theatre and Visual Arts:

www.nationalartsstandards.org

For 1994 National Standards for Music Education:

www.musicstandfoundation.org/images/National_Standards_-_Music_Education.pdf

www.old.philorch.org/sites/default/files/13-14-Nat-Arts-

For 2014 National Music Standards, The Re-Imagined Arts Standards:

www.nafme.org/my-classroom/standards/

www.nafme.org/my-classroom/standards/core-music-standards/

For 2014 National Music Standards, The Re-Imagined Arts Standards, PK-8:

www.nafme.org/wp-content/uploads/2014/11/2014-Music-Standards-PK-8-Strand.pdf

Acknowledgments

Over the course of my lifetime, many people have either given me instruction, believed in my ability to teach, or followed my guidance. As such, I have developed a deep appreciation for my role as music educator.

First, I am grateful to the principals who hired me and supported me for twenty-seven years in public school music education. You came to the concerts. You got me the supplies I needed. You valued my programs. And you inspired me to do my very best.

I am also grateful to the many, many students who have appreciated and benefited from my lessons and classes—including the students I am teaching now. You have enriched my life tremendously by showing up, trying, and improving. In later years, I often thought of you young students as a second set of grandchildren. You warmed me with your smiles, your cards, and your compliments. This book would not be possible without you.

The tone and tenor of this book comes from my years at Ithaca College during the 1960s. The faculty was a cohesive group of instructors who ardently believed in accuracy and excellence. Some of the principles in this book were drummed into me in their classes. I could not have asked for a better music education. Many of you have passed on, so it is my deep regret that you won't be able to read this book and celebrate your part in it.

I am grateful for the editorial staff of the FMEA's *Florida Music Director*, who published some of my early articles on general music in the mid-1990s. That's when I began speaking out about the importance of K-2 music in building strong secondary ensembles. You listened and put my ideas into print.

Thank you to the Piano School of New York City where I had the wonderful opportunity to train children and adults for five years during my retirement from public schools (2012 to 2017). The journal I kept about classroom observations became the impetus to begin writing books about music education—including this book in particular.

It's been my very good fortune to have Debra Scacciaferro as my personal writing editor for the past ten years. Deb, I've learned so much from you during our writing sessions. We have a wonderful working relationship. I couldn't have completed this book without you.

I would also like to mention Crystal Edwards, Katie Fortuna, and Nicole Sturk from Atlantic Publishing Group in Ocala, Florida, whose talents and professionalism made this publishing process a joyful and hassle-free experience.

And that brings me to my husband, Jim Gagnon. You are my cheerleader, confidant, and chief critic. You've put up with burnt dinners, late dinners, and no dinners on days when I was deep into this project. Your valuable insights helped shape this book. Thank you for believing in me. You're the best!

And last, I believe this project to improve education in the lower grades has been inspired and prompted by God, the Creator. When I look back on my life, it appears that many of my experiences in life prepared me to write this book. If not for Divine guidance, why else would I have been woken up so many times at 3 a.m. with ideas that sent me running for a pen and paper?

I am grateful for my gift of teaching. Grateful to have discovered writing. And grateful for the privilege of authoring this book.

About the Author

Barbara A. Moir, M. Ed. is a graduate of Ithaca College School of Music, Ithaca, New York. She holds a New York State Permanent Certificate for Vocal and Instrumental Music K-12. She earned her master's degree in Elementary Education from SUNY Cortland, New York with a specialty in reading and holds a New York State Permanent Certificate in Nursery, PreK through 6th Grade.

Barbara has taught in all areas of music education across all grades in New York and Florida for twenty-seven years. She has been an early childhood teacher in two private schools and has tutored ESL (English as a second language) students in Jackson Heights, Queens, New York.

More specifically, in the 1970s, she gave a presentation for the vocal methods classes at Ithaca College on her classroom management improvements for Manhattanville Music. She has presented songwriting workshops in Florida for the public. In the 1990s, she presented a general music workshop at the Florida State Music Convention and wrote several articles published in the FMEA's *Florida Music Director*.

In addition, in 2012, she taught instrumental lessons for The Piano School of New York City (five years) and developed evening adult piano courses for Ulster-Orange BOCES in Goshen, New York (five years).

Barbara is the past two-term president (2006-2010) of the Manhattan (NYC) Branch of the National League of American Pen Women (an or-

organization that supports professional women in music, art, and writing) and served on their national board in Washington, D.C.

Barbara still pursues her life-long love of oil painting and continues to give private music lessons at her home on the Jersey Shore, where she lives with her husband, Jim, and their two goldendoodles.

Additional Information

Look for helpful videos and downloadable classroom aides, especially about the Loop Counting Method and the Companion Words Script, on the author's website: www.artofreadingmusic.com

www.ingramcontent.com/pod-product-compliance
Lightning Source LLC
Chambersburg PA
CBHW070940230426
43666CB00011B/2499